Books, Media & the Internet

Children's Literature for Today's Classrooms

Books, Media & the Internet

Children's Literature for Today's Classrooms

edited by
Shelley S. Peterson,
David Booth & Carol Jupiter

PORTAGE & MAIN PRESS

© 2009 by Shelley Stagg Peterson, David Booth, and Carol Jupiter

All rights reserved. Except as noted, no part of this publication may be reproduced or transmitted in any form or by any means—graphically, electronic, or otherwise—without the prior written permission of the publisher.

Portage & Main Press gratefully acknowledges the financial support of the Province of Manitoba through the Department of Culture, Heritage, Tourism & Sport and the Manitoba Book Publishing Tax Credit and the Government of Canada through the Book Publishing Industry Development Program (BPDIP) for our publishing activities.

Printed and bound in Canada by Friesens

Cover and interior design by Relish Design Ltd.

PERMISSIONS

Page 42: Material from *Stanley's Party*, written by Linda Bailey, illustrated by Bill Slavin is used by permission of Kids Can Press Ltd., Toronto © 2003 Bill Slavin.

Pages 51 and 52: Cover images from *50 Below Zero* (1986), *Mud Puddle* (1979), *The Paper Bag Princess* (1980), *Pigs* (1989), *Stephanie's Ponytail* (1996), and *Thomas' Snowsuit* (1985), written by Robert Munsch, illustrated by Michael Martchenko, published by Annick Press. Used with permission.

Cover image from *Purple, Green, and Yellow* (1992), written by Robert Munsch, illustrated by Hélène Desputeaux, published by Annick Press. Used with permission.

Image of Robert Munsch courtesy of Annick Press. Reprinted with permission.

Page 169: Images from The Ontario Time Machine are provided courtesy of Toronto Public Library.

The Ontario Readers. First Reader, Part I. (Toronto: Canda Publishing Co., 1884) courtesy of the Kitchener Frontenac Public Library.

LIBRARY AND ARCHIVES CANADA CATALOGUING IN PUBLICATION

   Books, media, and the Internet: children's literature for today's classroom / edited by Shelley Stagg Peterson, David Booth and Carol Jupiter.

Includes bibliographical references.
ISBN 978-1-55379-203-1

   1. Literacy—Study and teaching—Computer-assisted instruction.
2. Literacy—Study and teaching—Technological innovations. 3. Children's literature—Study and teaching—Computer-assisted instruction.
4. Multicultural education—Computer-assisted instruction.
I. Booth, David W. (David Wallace), 1938- II. Peterson, Shelley
III. Jupiter, Carol

LB1575.B66 2009   372.64'0785   C2009-904076-X

Mixed Sources
Cert no. SW-COC-001271
© 1996 FSC

PORTAGE & MAIN PRESS

www.pandmpress.com

100–318 McDermot Ave.
Winnipeg, MB Canada R3A 0A2
Email: books@portageandmainpress.com
Toll-free: 1-800-667-9673
Fax-free: 1-866-734-8477

ENVIRONMENTAL BENEFITS STATEMENT

Portage and Main Press saved the following resources by printing the pages of this book on chlorine free paper made with 30% post-consumer waste.

TREES	WATER	SOLID WASTE	GREENHOUSE GASES
5 FULLY GROWN	2,239 GALLONS	136 POUNDS	465 POUNDS

Calculations based on research by Environmental Defense and the Paper Task Force. Manufactured at Friesens Corporation.

Contents

	Foreword *Shelley Stagg Peterson, David Booth, Carol Jupiter*	*vii*
Section One	**Reading Words and Images in Print and on Screen**	*1*
Chapter 1.	Literature in a New Era: Porous, Hybrid, Slippery, and Unfinished *Margaret Mackey*	*3*
Chapter 2.	Airheads, Brand Names, and the Lit. in Literacy *Deirdre Baker*	*11*
Section Two	**Engaging with Texts in Print and on Screen**	*21*
Chapter 3.	Debugging Texts with Metacognition *Carol Jupiter*	*23*
Chapter 4.	Power Up Picture Books *Kristin Main*	*37*
Chapter 5.	Scaffolding Early Literacy Using the SMART Board *Brenda Stein Dzaldov and Elana Shapiro Davidson*	*47*
Section Three	**Writing Our Way into Literature Using Multimedia and Digital Technology**	*57*
Chapter 6.	Being, Becoming, and Belonging: An Integrated Literacy Approach *Miriam Davidson and Mary Ladky*	*59*
Chapter 7.	Art-Full Journals: Making Multimodal Connections *Jane Baskwill*	*71*
Chapter 8.	Cyberwriters: Bringing Historical Fiction into the World of New Literacies *Jeanette Thompson*	*87*

Chapter 9.	Developing Agency and Voice: Radically Rewritten Traditional Tales *Heather Lotherington*	*97*
Section Four	**Critical Reading of Print and Non-Print Texts**	**107**
Chapter 10.	Using Traditional and Multimodal Texts to Promote Multicultural Literacy and Intercultural Connections *Jamie Campbell Naidoo*	*109*
Chapter 11.	The Lion, the Witch, and the Cereal Box: Reading Children's Literature across Multimedia Franchises *Naomi Hamer*	*121*
Chapter 12.	Toytexts: Critically Reading Children's Playthings *Linda Cameron and Kimberly Bezaire*	*137*
Section Five	**Libraries: Literature and the Internet**	**151**
Chapter 13.	What Are All the Computers Doing in the Public Library? *Ken Setterington*	*153*
Chapter 14.	Rare Books in the Classroom: Interactive Programs and Digital Collections of Historical Children's Books *Leslie McGrath*	*163*
Section Six	**Afterword**	**175**
Chapter 15.	Children's Literature and the New Literacies: What about assessment? *Shelley Stagg Peterson*	*177*
Chapter 16.	Read Me a Story, but Plug It in First *David Booth*	*183*
Appendix	**Teaching Tools**	**189**
	Getting to Know the Technology *Kristin Main*	*191*
	Using Microsoft Photo Story 3 *Shirley Sinclair*	*195*
	Contributors	*205*

Foreword

We are people of the book. But we do not wear blinkers. We are attuned to and, on a daily basis, employ the technological tools at our fingertips; for example, this book was written, revised, and edited using word-processing software on our computers. Email enabled us to communicate with our participating authors, our publisher, and each other. Truly, it saved us time and energy. Yet, despite these benefits, we often turn to books and appreciate the permanency of print on the page.

Our attachment to story and words may, in part, account for our love of books. It is hard to imagine reading a bedtime story to a child from a computer screen. We prefer the image of a child cuddled up with a parent, pointing to pictures, touching the page, and turning the pages back and forth to explore the illustrations in the book. But at some later point in time, that same child might take great delight in reading that book and others on screen, using a mouse to turn the pages, or listening to a voice emanating from the computer speakers reading the story. Behold the intersection of text and screen.

This interaction continues as we consider that the computer is often our default dictionary and encyclopedia, whether we're reading text on screen or on the printed page. The two formats work together as cross-references that inform and lead us to other books, more websites, and other media. In fact, *google* has taken pride of place as both noun and verb in everyday parlance.

Despite this electronic dominance and despite the predictions of many pundits, we see that books, magazines, and newspapers have not yet disappeared. We wonder why there are more books sold today at a time when there is an explosion of electronic texts. Why hasn't the world gone paperless? What is it about the iconic and ironic quality of the printed page that accounts for the continued existence of books in our wired world? We understand there is something unique about a book—sheets of paper printed with words and bound together—that somehow meets the mystical need to hold, carry, and commune with the text at one's own pace. These experiences are not far removed from first writing, the moment of pride when a child puts their first marks on paper and declares it a story. These are elemental events that mark our personal history. Would these be the same if confined to a simulated paper page on a computer?

While we ponder the role of technology in our literate lives, there are children throughout the world who clamour for books. In Margriet Ruurs's book *My Librarian Is a Camel: How Books Are Brought to Children around the World*, the book is a rare and expensive artefact. She regales us with tales of the ingenuity, the energy, and the lengths to which people have gone to deliver books into the welcoming arms of eager readers. Books come by camel, elephant, bicycle, and riverboat to remote communities where readers of all ages rush forth to gather up these treasures. We conjure up a picture that is in stark contrast to our own experience where books surround us in libraries and bookstores—there are volumes stacked on every available surface in many homes. Many of us adults could not imagine a life where books were not easily at hand.

Yet, in the world outside classrooms, books are losing their prominence in the lives of young people. After all, our students are comfortable in a texting, chatting, googling realm. Many young people appear to live life on screen. In fact, wireless libraries abound as universities put entire libraries on line. Hundreds of thousands of books are now a mere finger tap away. Our students no longer need to read *books*, that is, the artifacts.

But, like many educators and authors, we believe there is a place in today's classrooms for both literacies—reading the new digital and multimedia texts *and* reading traditional paper-based forms (books, magazines, and newspapers). We recognize that the worlds of paper and screen are not mutually exclusive, which is the thinking that led us to develop this book. Knowing that this reality was being addressed in classrooms around the globe, we invited prominent educators and researchers from two continents to present their research on children's literature in its many forms and guises at our conference called "A Place for Children's and Young Adult Literature in New Literacies Classrooms," held in Toronto, Ontario, in April 2008. The teaching ideas and stories presented then have been reworked for this book—they come from classrooms in Australia, Canada, and the United States.

Within the covers of this book, we have broken through the barricade that traditionally positioned reading teachers in one of two camps—text on screen versus text printed on paper. We show that, in children's lives, there are no walls between printed texts and on-screen texts. It's not a matter of one type of text making another obsolete; instead, students find that each type of text offers something that the other cannot. Digital and media texts should be used hand in hand with printed texts, not supplant them. As enthusiastic readers of children's literature in print, we have placed, and will continue to place, children's literature at the forefront of our teaching. Yet, we are also excited about the endless possibilities offered by media and digital texts.

This book "speaks" not only to the technologically capable and media-savvy teachers but also to those who are curious, who seek starting points to use technology and media *along with* the books in their classrooms. This book provides information, classroom examples, and anecdotes as practical tools to help teachers use digital, media, and print texts to extend students' learning.

The contributors

We have selected the work of the following authors to explore the nuances and the pitfalls of the myriad text forms that might fill our children's lives.

In Section One, "Reading Words and Images in Print and on Screen," we bring together two authorities on children's literature to present different views on texts for children. Margaret Mackey, professor of Library and Information Sciences at the University of Alberta, offers us a new vision of literature, contrasting the permanence of print with the ephemeral, slippery nature of electronic and hybrid texts. Deirdre Baker, professor of English at the University of Toronto, is a leading and widely read reviewer of children's literature. She writes about critically examining the influence of a consumer-driven society as reflected in young adult literature. Because a book is frozen in time, it lets us reflect on the ideas and frees us from what Ron Jobe calls "the web of immediacy." We bring these two thinkers together to highlight our vision of children's literature in the contemporary world. How will we as stewards of children's reading lives guide our children to an understanding of the new modes of meaning making? These two chapters reflect the contemporary issues facing all of us in today's electronic-media-saturated and book-filled environment. Mass media, readily manipulated and widely available digital texts, and books in both print form and on hand-held electronic readers testify to the complexity of children's literature at home and at school.

In Section Two "Engaging with Texts in Print and on Screen," Carol Jupiter, Kristin Main, Brenda Stein Dzaldov and Elana Shapiro Davidson present opportunities for involving young people in responding to and creating texts. In "Debugging Texts with Metacognition," Carol Jupiter reminds us that we can nudge children's comprehension of any text through mindful interactive questioning and teachers' think-alouds. She offers a checklist for assessing the literacy strategies that students use when making meaning with websites and literature. In "Power Up Picture Books," Kristin Main uses electronic game methodology to manipulate electronic images of picture book illustrations when interpreting and recreating meaning in intermediate classrooms. Similarly, in their chapter "Scaffolding Early Literacy Using the SMART Board," Brenda Stein Dzaldov and Elana Shapiro Davidson incorporate the technology of the SMART Board into the framework of a balanced literacy program for primary classrooms. In "Teaching Tools" at the end of this book, Kristin explains how to use a variety of digital tools in the classroom.

The authors in Section Three, "Writing Our Way into Literature Using Multimedia and Digital Technology," connect children's writing of media and digital texts to their reading of literature and other text forms.

In "Being, Becoming, and Belonging: An Integrated Literacy Approach," Miriam Davidson and Mary Ladky describe a project in an intermediate classroom where students use photography and a selection of literary texts to help students find their voices through poetry writing. Jane Baskwill, in "Art-Full Journals: Making Multimodal Connections," describes a project where students using digital and multimedia texts respond to media and print text sets, and connect to text through their own life experiences and through the arts (e.g., collage, drama and dance). Jen Thompson, in "Cyberwriters: Bringing Historical Fiction into the World of New Literacies," describes a writing project where young writers create historical fictional narratives using digital images, sounds, and words. In Teaching Tools, Jen Thompson's colleague, Shirley Sinclair, presents a recipe for creating photo stories. Heather Lotherington, in "Developing Agency and Voice: Radically Rewritten Traditional Tales," explores the possibilities for digitally retelling traditional fairy tales, folk stories, and fables by transforming them into individually published booklets, iMovies, and video games.

In Section Four, "Critical Reading of Print and Non-Print Texts," the authors move us into the social and cultural underpinnings of reading multicultural and intercultural books and media, as well as books that become media and toy texts. In Jamie Naidoo's chapter, "Using Traditional and Multimodal Texts to Promote Multicultural Literacy and Intercultural Connections," he uses international literature in different forms to deepen understanding between cultures. Naomi Hamer's chapter, "The Lion, the Witch, and the Cereal Box: Reading Children's Literature across Multimedia Franchises," highlights the cross-marketing of books, film, TV, music albums, video games, and clothing and provides forums for in-class reflection and discussion. Linda Cameron and Kimberly Bezaire's chapter, "Toytexts: Critically Reading Children's Playthings," looks at the role of toytexts derived from the media (television shows, video games, websites) that are marketed to children through a web of interrelated texts. The authors raise awareness of the behaviours and attitudes that arise as children are being manipulated without critical understanding.

In Section Five, "Libraries: Literature and the Internet," Ken Setterington and Leslie McGrath write about the technological resources of public libraries. Ken Setterington's chapter is a report on the new face of the public library where technology lives alongside print resources in providing our students with educational experiences beyond the classroom. Leslie McGrath introduces us to webquests and self-contained web-based programs that provide a free multidisciplinary resource for classrooms in her chapter "Rare Books in the Classroom! Interactive Programs and Digital Collections of Historical Children's Books."

In the "Afterword," Shelley Stagg Peterson writes about the challenge of assessing students' growth as literacy learners. David Booth concludes with a reflective essay, drawing together the modes of children's literature past and present.

A final word

We trust that you, the reader, will review and cogitate on all the text forms that engage our children and find your own ways of accommodating the varied shapes, sizes, and materials of children's literature so that each child will be able to know the solitude of a book, the excitement of an online inquiry, the involvement of hearing an author speak aloud on a webcast, the discovery of writings from around the world and, like our authors, declare themselves a lover of all texts.

Shelley Stagg Peterson
David Booth
Carol Jupiter
—JULY 2009

Section One

Reading Words and Images in Print and on Screen

Chapter 1

Literature in a New Era: Porous, Hybrid, Slippery, and Unfinished

Margaret Mackey

English Language Arts (ELA) curricula in Canada provide us with productive vocabulary for exploring how young people engage with literary materials. Through *listening* and *speaking*, *reading* and *writing*, *viewing* and *representing*, students are invited to connect with texts in both receptive and productive ways.

But there is a snag of increasing importance—those six terms suggest binary distinctions that, ironically, may not work so well in the Internet age. Peter Lunenfeld, in *Unfinished Business* (1999), refers to "the universal solvent of the digital" and this digital solvent, by merging what we have long thought of as distinctive activities, is shifting some of our basic cognitive frameworks.

In an age of digitization, textual possibilities are morphing, blurring, becoming less clear-cut. Today's artistic and communicative work is more porous, hybrid, slippery, and "unfinished" than ever before. What do these changes mean for our engagement with literature—and for the ways we teach literature?

In this chapter, I will not report on a single research project; rather, I will explore conclusions I have drawn from more than a decade of talking with readers and users of multimedia about their attitudes and behaviours, and relate these conclusions to contemporary literature teaching.

Porousness

The distinctions outlined in ELA curricula blur when we start to think about some of the digital options in our lives. Let us explore some of the fuzziness that marks contemporary communication, some of the ways our categories now permeate each other.

The division between writing and speaking, for example, loses some of its distinctiveness when we think about chatting, Instant Messaging, and texting. Like writing, these exchanges are created using a keyboard; like writing, they are recorded; but like speaking, they involve turn-taking in real time, and often the record is temporary.

Similarly, the distinction between viewing and writing becomes a little fuzzy in some television-related websites. In an online fan forum like *Television Without Pity*, for example, viewers write, sometimes even as they watch, to communicate with other viewers and with the show's producers. Sometimes the producers insert a "shout-out" in the program, speaking within the fabric of the story itself but addressing concerns raised on these websites.

Or, reading may bleed into representing. Look at the millions of *Harry Potter* websites. One response to J. K. Rowling's famous books is the website *Potter Puppet Pals*, who appear in short videos on YouTube. The pals comprise a set of finger puppets and, in their most famous work, "The Mysterious Ticking Noise," these puppets make a song out of the simple repetition of characters' names (technically an ostinato, a musical form that repeats basic motifs). Inevitably, there is now a parody of this parody; the soundtrack of "The Mysterious Ticking Noise" has been recast to accompany fast-changing images of the characters taken from films, book covers, advertising materials, and so forth. The original song is playful and appealing; the second-level parody draws our attention to the variable images we now associate with the names repeated in the song. To call it *reflective* would be a considerable stretch, but it does evoke some sense of the yoke of the proper noun in collecting plural images to represent a single character.

Viewing, representing, and a kind of speaking (singing) come together with the karaoke track on the DVD of *High School Musical*. By singing and dancing along, young viewers participate *as they view*, and become part of the fiction through their bodily action.

But it is not merely in the arena of fiction that such blurring occurs. Wikipedia, for example, offers opportunities to merge reading (researching) with writing (publishing). Online "sports bars" combine viewing with writing because fans

> are turning on the TV set [for the hockey game], then logging on to the computer and heading to sites and blogs devoted to [the home team]. Through the game, they engage in a running commentary—or game thread—where they immediately communicate their joy … or disgust (Staples 2007, A3).

Although this discussion takes place in writing, it shares qualities of speech in its instant references to events ("Did you see that??!!"—a comment incomprehensible outside the immediate context).

In short, the digital world dissolves some categories of action that until recently seemed self-evidently discrete. It may be time to revisit these curricular categories to explore how well they still serve us.

Hybridity

As a result of new, often digital, approaches to textual engagement, we are beginning to see new forms of text. *Machinima*, for example, are filmed stories created by means of digital game engines. Characters, settings, ways of moving and interacting are taken from the game and reworked into new stories, parodic or poignant. In a different example, the television program *csi* staged a program involving *Second Life*, the massively multiplayer online game. The game now houses a site where people can create avatars in the "skins" of characters from the television program *csi*, and develop their own plots and actions within that world (Riley 2007). Using the written word, fans become fiction authors as they create and publish online a variety of crossover stories that merge different story universes; other fans use images and music, not writing, to convey their responses to fictional universes.

Print has long represented stability. "What is a book?" asks Derrick de Kerckhove, and answers his question as follows:

> A resting place for words. It sounds trite, but in fact the printed page is the only place where words do have a rest. Everywhere else, they are moving; when you speak, when you see them on a screen, when you see them on the Net, words are moving. But a book is a restful place. The printed word is, and always was, still. (de Kerckhove 1997, 107).

But even print on paper is taking on hybrid qualities. Sean Stewart's new novel, *Cathy's Book* (2006), for example, contains print and pictures and is designed to offer a stylized representation of a teenager's notebook with doodles and graffiti. But the book also contains an envelope of artefacts—such as photos, memos, napkins with reminders written on them,—attached inside the front cover. Furthermore, it is embellished with telephone numbers that actually work (reaching a voicemail service) and live web addresses; in some ways, it resembles an alternate reality game, with the fiction overlapping onto real spaces in our world.

Television programs, for some time now, have linked to websites that provide embellishments and expansion materials from the story world. Books are beginning to try the same route to an audience. For example, even before they were adapted into a TV series, the Gossip Girl books also publicized a web connection that, at a minimum, rendered the abstractions of the print words more concrete and more vivid.

In a few experimental cases, creators have made a deliberate show of spreading a story across a variety of media. *The Matrix* supplied one famous example in the early 2000s when the Wachowski brothers produced a distributed story that was told in three movies, a videogame, short online animations on the Internet, comic books, and a massively multiplayer online game, all contributing to the same story world. To gain access to the complete story, viewers were required to explore all these sites. In the case of *The Matrix*, the distribution of the story was deliberate and planned from the outset, but many other fictional universes have acquired web add-ons through a process of accretion. When the *Degrassi* television series began, it was largely confined to the small screen, but over the years web additions have expanded on aspects of the drama.

Slipperiness

It is possible to consider collecting and assembling the distributed pieces of *The Matrix* into one more or less coherent whole. But some contemporary stories are "shiftier" than that—there is no single authoritative narrative. Kristie Fleckenstein (2003) talks about "slippery texts" that are designed to evolve and mutate like the massively multiplayer online role-playing games in which fictional universes are created and expanded by the players. Some of these games are so large that they run on more than one server and evolve at the behest of their players into different but related worlds, no one of which bears higher authority than the others.

Pokémon has for many years sustained a fictional world where mutation is part of the framework. Players own and trade cards and play out intricate scenarios in games involving these cards. The provision of backstory for each character is one way in which this fictional world is furnished with narrative coherence, but the idiosyncrasies of individual games are equally important.

It would be easy enough to claim that *Pokémon* fails any reasonable litmus test of literary quality, and I would certainly not label it a literary experience. What it undoubtedly does, however, is expand children's ideas of how fiction works, what rules make it possible to assemble a fictional understanding—and these expanded ideas have an impact on how children approach all their stories.

An aesthetic of unfinish

"Technology and popular culture," says Peter Lunenfeld, "propel us toward a state of unfinish in which the story is never over, and the limits of what constitutes the story proper are never to be as clear again" (1999, 14).

In a world of adapting, reworking, branding, digitizing, and mutating, "unfinish" is the name of the game. The movie of *The Golden Compass* offers a very interesting example. The book on which this film is based was first published a dozen years ago, and a wonderful unabridged audio version soon followed; the official website for the book was an early example of how the web can expand on a fictional universe. The adaptation staged at London's National Theatre was breathtaking in its ambition.

The branding exercise for the film, however, was all too familiar. Trailers, leaks to chosen blogs, teaser interviews with actors and directors gave way to merchandising—toys, gadgets, picture books, poster books, paper dolls, novelizations, screenplays, and *Golden Compass* board and video games.

The movie raised quite real and diverse questions of unfinish. As it opened widely in late 2007, the producers stressed that the two sequels would be filmed if and only if the box office figures for this first venture were sufficiently astonishing. So the issue of unfinish, temporarily at least, included a genuine question mark about whether or how the remainder of the story would be told. Television viewers are familiar with this kind of suspension, but it added a new frisson of unfinish to Philip Pullman's saga.

Other components of unfinish are also marked in the adaptations of this particular story. The ending of the book is famous for its bitter treachery and its resolute turning to new adventures. As Lyra and her daemon head for new worlds at the end of the story, the echo-chamber created by the turning of the final page lets that ending resonate in our minds, at least until we can lay our hands on the sequel. Interestingly, both stage play and movie sacrifice that combination of the epic moment of resolution followed by the silence of the end of the story. The stage play, by turning three novels into two three-hour plays, places Lyra's departure from her own world midway through the second half of the first play, and the action of the drama continues apace. The movie chooses to end the story three chapters before the end of the book.

The question of unfinish here has deep commercial roots. Director Chris Weitz said "his decision to end the movie earlier in the narrative had been influenced by the need for a more box-office-friendly happy ending to establish the foundation for what he hopes will be a film trilogy" (Collett-White 2007, B13). Author Pullman seems happy to place the tumultuous scenes of Lyra's betrayal at the beginning of the second movie, partly in hopes of encouraging that second movie to be made.

> What a good idea to end the film like that. It's quite the best place to stop. The book is fine as it is, but the opening of the second film would be a much better place for the complex, ambiguous drama of the last chapter; and it was much more likely that the second film would be made if the first one ended on a clear, strong and immediately understandable note (Pullman 2007).

Ironically, therefore, "unfinish" grants licence for those reworking the story to turn away from the stunning lack of closure that makes the book's conclusion so resonant. It is a reminder that even the most artistically choreographed ending can be unpicked and reworked in this era of unfinish.

It is not just the branding exercises that accompany film adaptation that make ours an era of unfinish, however. Fan activities likewise assault firmly established conclusions and open them up to new kinds of story-making. Characters have new adventures, move into other fictional worlds, change gender or sexual orientation, and otherwise mutate in fan creations. And any digital creation is always open to reworking by its very nature. For example, one fan was irritated enough by the conclusion to *The Golden Compass* to write a different ending:

> Lyra knew you were never to touch another's daemon.
> However, Lyra knew what was about to happen to Roger, and under the circumstances, she wasn't about to just wait for [sic]. With such strength that it even left her to tumble into the snow, her boot came into contact with Stelmaria's head....
> She *would* learn about Dust. And she *would* get to that other world. And she *would* have Roger by her side doing it. (Fan Fiction)

Readers have always been free to re-imagine or rewrite stories that displease them in some way, but the power to put that alternative story into the public domain alters the balance of power between author and reader in subtle and fluid ways. One intriguing question is whether all readers feel that shift, or whether awareness of such a change is confined to fan writers.

Conclusions

The students who walk through any ELA classroom door today, in any part of the Western world at least, are at home with porousness, hybridity, slipperiness, and unfinish. What does this development mean for how we think about the teaching of literature?

If we take the works of Shakespeare as an exemplar for discussing classroom practice, we can readily observe that these functions are not entirely new. But Shakespeare's fluid attitude to historical material, literary form, definitive print editions (including received spelling), and the urge to rework is not reproduced and enacted inside many classrooms. Despite the nebulousness of what we actually know about his final opinion on any particular play, the playscript that is actually *studied* in the classroom is usually reified and treated as a relatively closed text.

If we take the leap of opening up the texts we teach, we may find that students are well ahead of us in terms of being able to think of all literary choices as plastic and reworkable. If we look carefully at what is gained by introducing ideas of porousness, hybridity, slipperiness, and unfinish, we may better place ourselves to hold the counterbalancing conversation about what is also lost. We may open the door to critical debate about how choices are made, who gets to make them, and what kinds of consequences ensue from one choice or another. We may find ways of moving the sorts of critical understanding often best developed in the classroom into an exploration of decisions made in the alternative cultural universes inhabited by many of our students. But that discussion will be most fruitful if we acknowledge that critical understanding is a two-way street, and that the changing world of popular culture also provides us with new tools of understanding and evaluation.

Who gets to dictate and control the terms of unfinish? Is it the take-charge teacher ("You may only come back to open up the book on my educational terms, to explore and critique"), the fan fiction-writing reader ("I'm going to remake this story to suit me"), the commercial brander

("We see ways of making more money out of this story")? What role is played by a larger and more amorphous form of collective interaction with porous, hybrid, and slippery stories?

If we fail to address these questions, they will not disappear from our classrooms. They will remain, perhaps unvoiced, in the minds of our students and will serve to undermine our authority when we speak about texts as "closed and finished." Teachers who address these questions will join their classes in investigating some of the radical changes in contemporary culture, an exciting and dynamic prospect.

REFERENCES

Collett-White, Mike. 2007, December 1. "Pullman film under fire for attack on religion." *Edmonton Journal*, B13.

de Kerckhove, Derrick. 1997. *Connected intelligence: The arrival of the web society*. Toronto: Patrick Crean/Somerville House.

Fleckenstein, Kristie S. 2003. *Embodied literacies: Imageword and a poetics of teaching*. Studies in Writing and Rhetoric. Carbondale: Southern Illinois University Press.

Lunenfeld, Peter. 1999. "Unfinished business." In *The Digital Dialectic: New Essays on New Media* (ed. Peter Lunenfeld). Cambridge MA: MIT Press, 6–22.

Pullman, Philip. 2007, December 2. "My Golden Compass sets a true course." *Sunday Times*, <http://entertainment.timesonline.co.uk/tol/arts_and_entertainment/film/article2982762.ece> (accessed March 21, 2009).

Riley, Duncan. 2007, October 20. "*CSI: NY* comes to *second life* Wednesday." *TechCrunch*, <http://www.techcrunch.com/2007/10/20/csiny-comes-to-second-life-wednesday/> (accessed March 21, 2009).

Staples, David. 2007, December 3. "Oilers fans share play by play in online 'sports bars'." *Edmonton Journal*, A3.

RESOURCES

Websites

Television without Pity, <http://www.televisionwithoutpity.com/index.php> (accessed March 21, 2009).

"The Mysterious Ticking Noise," <http://www.youtube.com/watch?v=Tx1XIm6q4r4> (accessed March 21, 2009). Parody can be found at <http://www.youtube.com/watch?v=_Hk6qyeYjIY&feature=related> (accessed March 21, 2009).

The Matrix in a variety of media: <http://en.wikipedia.org/wiki/The_Matrix_series> (accessed March 21, 2009).

Fan Fiction: Friendship <http://www.fanfiction.net/s/3941878/1/Friendship> (accessed March 20, 2009).

The *Degrassi* series, <http://www.the-n.com/ntv/shows/index.php?id=67> (accessed March 21, 2009).

The Golden Compass, official website for the book <http://www.randomhouse.com/features/pullman/books/golden_compass.html> (accessed March 21, 2009).

Chapter 2

Airheads, Brand Names, and the Lit. in Literacy

Deirdre Baker

In its root, *literacy* is a word that pertains to text, but it has now accrued broader, more figurative meanings: *literacy* is no longer only about decoding the little black marks. "Just don't forget who taught you to read," Tycho Potter warns his friend and soon-to-be lover Angela in *The Catalogue of the Universe* by Margaret Mahy. "I could read ages before I started talking to you," Angela replies. "Yes, but you didn't know what you were reading," Tycho says. Literacy is about "knowing what you are reading" (Mahy 1986, 125) and that is what, as teachers, we aim to help our students do.

Expressive language is one way we judge literacy—it shows the ability to manipulate language and is predicated on understanding it. With respect to literature and reading, a passive way we ingest language, literacy means learning to discern or recognize how language is being manipulated. To understand how language is being manipulated, we have to understand not only that there is another way to say this but also that conveying it another way would make a difference, obvious or subtle, to its meaning or to its effect on the reader.

Literacy of this kind is close to understanding rhetoric—the vocabulary, phrasing, and tricks of expression we use to sway someone to our point of view, to hide a truth without lying, or to create a dramatic effect. It is relevant not only to what we think of as literature or literary fiction but also to any sort of writing or speaking—journalism, news reports, song lyrics, political speeches, advertisements, and even those printouts we get from the pharmacist when we pick up our prescriptions. This kind of literacy means "being able to see through things."

Many of our students have literacies that we teachers don't. Most of them are far more versed in pop culture and hip fashion than we are. They bring to the Gossip Girl novels, for example, a finely honed consumer savvy that informs and enhances their appreciation of what's going on in the story. I would like to show that we can take what seems a very non-literary, bottom-line kind of literacy —that is, brand name recognition— and, by following it through a number of young adult novels, usher our students from reflecting on market literacy through to a literary appreciation that depends on recognizing what language can and does do, with or without brand names. From the ridiculous—Cecily von Ziegesar's *Gossip Girl*—to the sublime—Tim Wynne-Jones's *Rex Zero: King of Nothing*.

I also want to stress that our students' literacy is radically contingent upon our own. If we are going to teach children and adolescents, we must be thoroughly familiar with children's and young adult literature. It is only through familiarity with a broad range of what's available in that literature—contemporary and otherwise—that we will be able to choose texts to juxtapose and compare in ways that surprise, astonish, and captivate our students…ways that seduce them, in fact, to the pleasures of reading.

Let us begin with Cecily von Ziegesar's hugely popular Gossip Girl books, a series that revolves around a cluster of mostly wealthy teenagers who attend exclusive private schools in Manhattan, New York. It sparked controversy when *The New York Times* published an article by Naomi Wolf, who lamented the banality of its writing style, but especially of its characters and plots. The main characters are vapid, mean, and arrogant; better feelings don't win out; and brand name fashion dominates the description. No one wears just a pair of jeans: we have to know the make and where they were purchased. Indeed, von Ziegesar uses brand names in a way so crass that, for sophisticated readers, it is parodic. For the average everyday reader, however, it is probably not parodic.

The Gossip Girl book I picked up is *You're the one that I want*, the volume in which the characters, at the end of their last year of high school, learn the results of their college applications. In this passage, spoiled rich kid Blair is being given a tour of Georgetown University by one of its undergraduates, Rebecca:

> Rebecca beamed up at Blair through thick, blue-mascaraed lashes. Her permed, bleached-blond hair smelled of Finesse hair products, and her white leather Reeboks were so new they looked like they'd never been worn outside the mall.
>
> Blair flicked a stray hair off the sleeve of her new pink Marni suit jacket. "I need to book a hotel room for tonight —" (von Ziegesar 2004, 88).

If we present this to students, what should we expect them to make of it? First, let's think about the connotations of the brand names. Here, *literacy* means *market and fashion literacy*. Rebecca, a Georgetown undergrad, washes her hair with Finesse and wears Reeboks. Blair, a wealthy private-school student from Manhattan who hoped to get into Yale but was accepted by Georgetown, wears a pink Marni suit jacket. A pink Marni suit jacket from the current online boutique costs £505 sterling. Finesse hair products are available anywhere at bargain prices, and Rebecca's Reeboks were probably purchased at a Prime Outlet Mall at a deep discount.

Brand names and labels are the way Von Ziegesar codes her characters. The gap between the two girls' economic status is obvious. The brands also indicate something about taste and character—Rebecca is lowbrow and Blair is highbrow—and the non-branded information we get is as important to our judgment as the brands. To say "so new they looked like they'd never been worn outside the mall" associates Rebecca with a suburban mall (we already know Blair shops in Manhattan) and their garish newness with suburban fashion, that is, in the narrator's eyes, bad fashion—Rebecca is tacky. The inelegant "thick, blue-mascaraed eyelashes" and "permed, bleached-blond hair" in conjunction with the Finesse hair products and Reeboks show us where to place Rebecca on the scale of desirability, taste, and intelligence. Cool Blair, by contrast, is shown "flicking a stray hair" off her sleeve—she knows when one should have hair around and when not. And to give von Ziegesar her due, this forgettable little passage sets us up for a major hair event in which Blair gets drunk, passes out, and wakes to find her legs brutally shaved and her hair dyed yellow—probably by Rebecca.

There's something else to notice here, and that's von Ziegesar's dependence on what we see. The actions she describes—Rebecca beaming; Blair flicking a hair—try to indicate something about the characters (Rebecca's over-enthusiasm; Blair's lack of it). Mostly, though, they are script-like cues, actions we expect because they confirm the stereotypes these girls are, stereotypes that are visible through the labels they wear.

Von Ziegesar uses brand names with a kind of hostility; in fact, you could make a persuasive argument that the Gossip Girl novels are works of hostility, and their huge sales are confirmation of all that von Ziegesar might be hostile toward or cynical about. If students are into this series, why not get them to analyze the function of brand names in any given paragraph? Let them do their own research in the marketplace of fashion and analyze the nuances (if any) of character and the application of brand. Get them to consider who is calling the shots in a Gossip Girl novel. From whose or what perspective do the brand names fall into place? Is there meaning to be drawn from the oddly empty arc of plot and character, and its matrix of brand name fashion? Finally, let the students think about what it means that they are seen walking the court of their own mall with *Gossip Girl* in hand.

The Gossip Girl series and similar series use brand names in a particularly glaring, purposefully in-your-face way. Now let's turn to a different popular story, one that includes almost as many names from the marketplace as Gossip Girl—Meg Cabot's *The Princess Diaries*. "He crushed my modem with a magnum of Châteauneuf du Pape," Mia remembers of one altercation with her father (Cabot 2000, 77). Here, as in the Gossip Girl novels, the brand name indicates economic status and taste—Mia's father is crown prince of Genovia; he's wealthy and cultured. But the way the label functions in this line is more complicated than that because whatever we might associate with Châteauneuf du Pape, an expensive and delicious wine, is at odds with Mia's father's employment of the bottle as a bludgeon wielded in a fit of paternal rage. The wedding of these incongruent notions results in a moment of humour and irony that is achieved by precise language. It tells us something about Mia, the narrator—her faux-naïve ironic voice works partly because it is so intelligent—and also about her father. How would the effect of this line change if Cabot had written instead: "he crushed my modem with a big bottle of wine"?

The word "magnum" also helps to make the line sharp—conveying Mia's father's expansiveness, excess even, and fourteen-year-old Mia's surprising familiarity with the vocabulary of wine bottles. Notice too, the rhythm and echo of "modem/magnum" at the centre of the line—two words one does not expect to see together—and the framing "crushed/Châteauneuf du Pape," incongruously balancing one another and drawing attention to the strangeness of it all. In its very sound, "crushed"—a strong, onomatopoeic monosyllable—contrasts with the more lyric rhythm of "Châteauneuf du Pape," creating yet another spark of comedy.

Cabot's use of brand names—labels, restaurants, grocery stores—is more buoyant than von Ziegesar's. "That's right. I got sent to the principal's office for stabbing Lana Weinberger with a Nutty Royale!" Mia writes in outrage later in the story. (Cabot 2000, 161) It's not just that her weapon was an ice cream cone, but that it was a Nutty Royale—as if a Drumstick or a Popsicle would have been a different matter. This incident recalls the earlier reference to Châteauneuf du Pape as a blunt instrument; once again, the associations with the weapon (sweet, delightful, trivial) are at odds with its use (rage, destruction). Notice, too, that it is a "nutty royal," just like Mia. She has stabbed Lana with herself. Cabot's use of, choice of, brands thus folds in layers of meaning and humour.

Like von Ziegesar, but less repetitively, Cabot also establishes character through brand association. Mia, for example, chooses to wear Converses and Doc Martens, not the Gucci shoes her grandmère forces upon her. For our student, the question is what exactly do Converses and Doc Martens mean? Or Gucci shoes, aside from the obvious element of expense? What assumptions or perhaps cultural literacy do our students bring to bear in interpreting these allusions? An examination of brand names in Cabot's novels or in the Gossip Girl series is not only a way for students to analyze writing but also for them to examine the nuances of image-making that they themselves employ in their own dress and pop cultural associations. In *The Princess Diaries* also, brand labels can be a way for students to consider irony and how it works.

Brand names provide built-in obsolescence because brands and fashion are exceptionally volatile. We can make use of such ephemera by giving students passages from stories set in earlier eras; for example, Edith Nesbit's *The Story of the Treasure Seekers* with its references to Victorian advertising; Martha Brooks's *Two Moons in August* with its allusions to the Jantzen bathing suits of the 1950s; Tim Wynne-Jones's *Rex Zero and the End of the World* with its references to commodities of the 1960s. What were once household words are now objects of historical study. Simply identifying them involves research, never mind retrieving whatever connotations of class, taste, or finances they might have. For this reason, while they might be used as a way to set the period of a novel—as they are in Tim Wynne-Jones's Rex Zero stories—in the most enduring literature, they are not essential to character or plot.

Take, for example, Tim Wynne-Jones's *Rex Zero: King of Nothing*. In the following passage, Rex's family, which includes his mother, father, and four sisters (Cassie, Letitia, Annie Oakley, and Flora Bella) as well as his baby brother, the Sausage (otherwise named Rupert), have a family dinner that includes for the first time Mr. Brian Odsburg, Cassie's sweetheart. Mr. Odsburg works in a department store, and he has just been promoted out of the china department to be the new manager of precious jewels:

> "Like diamonds?" says Letitia.
> "Yes, diamonds," says Mr. Odsburg. "Diamonds, emeralds, sapphires."
> "Lovely," says Mum. "When I was young, we had a cat named Opal."
> "Mother," says Cassie. "Opals are only semi-precious."
> "Well, she wasn't a very nice cat."
> "Is that the one I ran over?" asks Dad.
> Mum stops serving the lamb roast for a moment and then smiles.
> "Why, yes. I think it was. In the Austin?"
> Dad nods.
> "Now that, my man, was a real car."
> Mr. Odsburg has a piece of potato almost to his mouth but he's forced to put it down in order to reply.
> "Yes, sir. I've heard good things about the Austin. They're difficult to buy here."
> "More's the pity," says Dad.
> "Brian has a Nash," says Cassie.
> "Have you tried Calmitol?" asks Mum. "It will take away the itch."
> "A Nash, Mother. Not a rash."
> "A 1952 Nash Rambler Country Club two-door hard-top," says Mr. Odsburg.
> "I don't believe it!" says Annie Oakley, bringing her fists down on the table.
> "It's true," says Cassie. "It's black, with a red interior."
> "I'm not talking about that," says Annie. "Didn't anybody hear what Daddy said? He said he drove over a cat." (Wynne-Jones 2007, 112–13)

The brand names in this exchange certainly establish the period in which the story takes place. The Austin, Nash Rambler, and Calmitol strike a chord with readers of the generation that might remember them. A little nostalgia. But Wynne-Jones's story is not primarily about the marketplace, and brand names are incidental to what gives the passage its energy and comic substance—the characterization of family members through idiosyncratic tangents; a counterpoint that hinges on the sort of family history and word associations we might see in any close family at any time. The insane, oblique logic and the family dynamic presented here can never be dated.

Analyzing humour often kills it but, even so, trying to articulate Wynne-Jones's moves will enhance the literacy of any student. First there's the move from precious jewels to the cat named Opal, a living being, the closest the mother can come to relating to jewels, since she has neither the class nor economic status to have enjoyed them herself. Cassie's correction, that opals are only semi-precious, is funny because instead of pointing out the most obvious irrelevance—that cats and diamonds don't belong in the same conversation—she picks on the least germane point, showing a way of thinking that is not unlike her mother's. The father's question, "Is that the one I ran over?" evokes a tragic history, a death, and a scene of emotional mayhem now past that is at odds with the innocent, even bland, topic that began the conversation, Mr. Odsburg's job in a department store. In the next line, it is not that the Austin, per se, is identified as the murder weapon, but that the car's make rather than the cat's death is mentioned, which provokes a laugh. Similarly, it is not that Mr. Odsburg drives a Nash Rambler that conveys meaning, but that the mother mishears "rash" for "Nash." Her response is motherly and nurturing, but her reference to an unromantic and all too bodily problem is a comic contrast to the discussion of cars. It also moves the focus from a showpiece of masculine power and sexiness (the car) to an embarrassing bodily experience that is decidedly un-erotic (itchiness).

This passage is full of possibilities for literary thinking. What does it convey about each participant's character, and how? Questions about pacing and timing, about irony and comic misapprehension arise naturally from the exchange. Brand names recede and give way to what makes any piece of writing always relevant—human character. Wynne-Jones is writing for readers who have no firsthand familiarity with his cultural allusions, but he does not depend on his audience for the market literacy that *Gossip Girl* demands; instead he offers something rich, nuanced, and timeless.

The volatility of fashion is part of the reason that we, as teachers, might find it hard to keep up our brand name and pop culture literacy, but the issues of consumerism and status-by-material-culture are, like the puzzle that is human nature, constant. In *Rex Zero*, we see a movement away from using brand names to command attention, and a greater focus on what is going on between the lines, between the characters. In M. T. Anderson's *Feed*, we have a novel that faces consumerism, name-branding, and the language of advertising head-on, but does so by using brand names that are entirely invented. It is partly their very "inventedness" that allows Anderson's portrait of consumer culture to be an exploration of how it affects human character and society, an exploration that leaves our minds buzzing with new apprehensions and insights.

In *Feed*, people are wired with continuous "feed," a full-time Internet connection and instant messaging service implanted in the brain in infancy. The feed tailors itself to one's interests as one chooses what to listen to and buy, where to holiday, and so on. It creates a market profile as one grows. "The braggest thing about the feed," claims Titus, the teenaged narrator, "the thing that made it really big, is that it knows everything you want and hope for, sometimes before you even know what those things are. It can tell you how to get them, and help you make buying decisions that are hard..." (Anderson 2002, 40)

Anderson mimics the rhythms, buzz words, and rhetorical devices of advertising and of our current popular media. His expression of the degradation of language is vivid, energetic, and original. It shows readers just how attention to the banalities of expression can be turned into something hair-raising, hilarious, and heart-breaking. Here is one excerpt from the book:

> ...if you liked "I'll Sex You In," you'll love these other popular slump-rock epics by the new storm n'chunder band Beefquake, full of riffs that....
> ...We handpicked our spring fashions...
> ...Hardgore, the best feed-sim battle game ever to rip up the horizon. Sixty levels of detonation and viscera just waiting to fly at your command, Captain Bastard. If you don't feel slogging waist-deep within fifteen seconds, we'll eat our fucking hats... (Anderson 2002, 59).

Slump-rock epics, storm n' chunder, a band called Beefquake, sixty levels of detonation and viscera—it is comic, but close to reality. What is the difference between this and ska, steampunk, or the names of any number of current bands? Such language points out the ephemeral nature of trend, or fashion, and also slyly illuminates the earnestness with which we adopt dumb terminology and commit ourselves to bizarre fads. In the broken phrases of this excerpt from *Feed*, Anderson echoes the phrasing and constructions of "real world" advertising: "...if you liked...you'll love..." Or, "Sixty levels of detonation and viscera just waiting to fly at your command..." a phrase in which the big number, sixty, is set right at the beginning of the sentence to attract attention by quantity. One can just hear the full rich male voice of current movie trailers proclaiming these with exaggerated dramatic emphasis. The very incompleteness of these bits of advertising, working on the reader as channel-surfing on television or radio might do, effectively conveys the hollowness and inconsequentiality of their content.

The real and contemporary labels with which *Gossip Girl* is peppered evolved, in *Feed,* into goods such as Weatherbee and Crotch's "trim-shirt with side pockets" that Titus "would have bought, except it only came in sand, persimmon and vetch." (Anderson 2002, 42) Vetch, retch, one cannot help thinking; but still, these colours could be lifted straight from a current catalogue from Abercrombie & Fitch. Even the real world brands in *Feed* are parodied in Anderson's invention of fascinating new products such as the "Nike speech tattoo" that Titus's friend Marty acquires. "[It's] pretty brag," Titus says. "It [means] that every sentence, he automatically [says] "Nike" (Anderson, 218). Here, brand name and obscenity are conflated, making a comic devastating critique of our culture's obscene consumerism.

Feed is a vision of what a generation of readers of the Gossip Girl books—not to mention consumers of the culture it springs out of and feeds into—will become. By slightly altering brand names and advertising language, by putting inane, clichéd expressions into a new context, Anderson compels his readers to think critically and analytically about language and consumerism. We can read Titus's story *only* in the light of what it parodies; we cannot avoid recognizing the degradation of language and thinking that Anderson puts before us. He jump-starts his readers into literacy, making them conscious of how we put things and why, which in turn points out that *there is another way to say this*—so why did he choose this one? The possibilities for discussion of market and literary literacy in *Feed* are, seemingly, endless.

Labels and brand names are one way we arouse desire—the thirst for acquisition, the seductive power of property, the pleasure of identifying with a character who has, and has, and has. In Anderson and in Wynne-Jones, the inclusion of brand names jars us out of unreflective participation in our consumer culture. In *Gossip Girl* and *The Princess Diaries*, we make that leap with the help of critical analysis. The very differences in the strategies of these writers can help us take our students more deeply into abstract literary matters—just as the strategy of "characterization by property" can lead us into the depths of cultural criticism or to Marx's theories of property and culture, a venture into matters political, philosophical, and literary.

Brand names are one way to start students thinking about a piece of literature that is, at first glance, unpromising. But we could turn back to the Gossip Girl books, start again, and use them for a different purpose. After all, it isn't only the brand names that cause critics to consider it pernicious reading—it's the sentences. It's the predictability of the language; the flat, conventional ways of getting the plot from here to there; the effect of words that are prevented from meaning more than the teeniest, weeniest bit that they could mean; it's the suppression of questions. It's the way it might encourage literary anorexia.

But that is another avenue into literacy. All I mean to suggest is that by following a thread such as the brand names through these stories, by exercising voracious curiosity and relentless questioning and an unstoppable commitment to reading literature for the young, each of us can find the stories, chapters, paragraphs, and words that will make our students take notice. We can spark their interests, whatever they are, and make thoughtful, critical interpretation irresistible and fun.

REFERENCES

Anderson, Matthew Tobin. 2002. *Feed*. Cambridge MA: Candlewick Press.
Cabot, Meg. 2000. *The princess diaries*. New York: HarperCollins Publishers.
Green, John. 2006. *An abundance of Katherines*. New York: Penguin, Dutton Children's Books.
Mahy, Margaret. 1986. *The catalogue of the universe*. New York: Atheneum.
Von Ziegesar, Cecily. 2004. *You're the one that I want*. New York: Little, Brown.
Wynne-Jones, Timothy. 2007. *Rex Zero: King of nothing*. Toronto: Groundwood Books.

Section Two

Engaging with Texts in Print and on Screen

Chapter 3

Debugging Texts with Metacognition
Carol Jupiter

>My old typewriter used to make so much noise
>I had to put a cushion of newspaper beneath it late at night
>so as not to wake the whole house (Collins 2002, 21).

The rhythmic clatter and ping have disappeared, but not the need to communicate and understand. This need to make and get meaning is the drive that keeps us swimming in an ocean of print and electronic media. To that end, we employ our metacognitive skills to bring us to meaning. But metacognition does not come out of the ether; like all skills, it needs to be taught and practised.

Donald Leu and his colleagues (2004) assure us that our ability to access new literacies is compromised if solid foundational literacies are not in place. This means that readers must be able to decode, comprehend, infer, have a strong vocabulary, and respond in writing. Simply put, these are the goals of all literacy instruction. Unfortunately, despite what publishers and researchers would have us believe, there is no formula to achieve this.

However, we do know what accomplished readers do. They
- think about the words and their meaning
- predict and confirm their predictions
- infer
- think about ideas contained in the text and how they connect within and without the text
- wonder
- ask themselves questions
- ask why
- reread to clarify

In sum, they are actively engaged in the process of reading. They call forth the techniques that enable them to address the meaning of the text. This ability to use techniques is metacognition, that is, thinking about thinking and learning about learning (Leu, Kinzer, Coiro, & Cammack 2004). Sounds powerful and simple, but how do we ensure that our students have—and employ—these skills? Once I had posed this question, my quest for an answer began.

Working with narrative texts

For my comfort and theirs, I began with a book. I decided to preface my reading to my students with a brief explanation of what accomplished readers do, which includes the skills bulleted in the previous paragraph. This gave them some insight into the complexities of reading.

I read the story *Wild Cameron Women* (Hull & Mills 2000) from beginning to end. The story tells us of Kate's night fears and how her Nana comes to solve the problem with Cameron plaid nightgowns, and told a story about Kate's ancestor who had special words to shout at the bears that emerged from her cupboard. I did not ask for predictions or confirmations. This was meant to be our time for simple enjoyment, the initial foray into new territory. I had multiple motives for this approach. Not only did I want them to listen to the words and interpret them, I also wanted them to be consciously aware of the process of interpreting. Furthermore, underlying everything was a desire to improve comprehension and to address higher-level thinking skills.

The second day I told them I was going to read the same story to them, but in a different way. I explained that, to help students understand what readers do, I would talk about my thinking while I read. This was not as easy as it sounds. First of all, I did not want this reading to sound contrived. Therefore, I did not predetermine what or where in the text I would discuss my thoughts. Instead I plunged in, but with one significant proviso—I consciously made myself aware of what I was thinking, questioning, wondering, and connecting while reading. This was somewhat challenging with an audience of 23 sitting at my feet. Despite the odds, it worked.

While sharing my thinking, I also had to get them involved. While they listened, they needed to be engaged in a similar textual probing. I invited them to do so with, "What are your thoughts?" They were hesitant at first, but the repeated opportunities resulted in increased participation and dialogue within the group.

How did this differ from other reading experiences? I didn't ask questions; instead, I introduced my thinking with leads such as

- I wondered…
- I noticed…
- I was confused…
- I was surprised…
- I think that the author…
- I felt…
- I disliked…

- I liked…
- I could see the story happening….

These open-ended leads encouraged them to speculate and share. Contradictory opinions were expressed, but none were discounted. The resultant discussion was a sharing of thoughts and impressions during which the children began to address each other directly. This sharing meant that most of the time it wasn't necessary for me to filter and redirect. The conversation flowed just as it does when adults talk about a book that they have read. It was delightful.

The following is a small sample of the conversations (all names are pseudonyms):

I began, "I wonder why Kate's parents called another adult, Nana, to ask for help in solving a problem."

Karen: "They were too tired."

Eve: "Yes, but they knew Nana had good ideas."

Tom: "Nana was really good at stories. She made the Kate in the story just like the real Kate."

Me: "Can you explain more of your idea?"

Tom: "Both Kates had red hair. Kate had tea and an oatmeal cookie at the teashop. In the story the seven greats-grandma Kate had the same things."

Susan: "So you're saying Nana made up the story to be just like Kate because she knew what Kate liked."

Tom: "Yes."

Although Karen's answer was straight from the text, Eve understood that there was much more involved. She stepped outside the text and inferred that Nana had more to offer. Tom paid attention to detail and created a visual image of Kate that enabled him to link the child Kate to the story Kate. Susan followed with her interpretation of Tom's comment. She intuited that Nana's story was contrived to help Kate overcome her night fears.

The children were pointing out parallels in structure, questioning the veracity of the story's premise, developing an understanding of the magnitude of the story's problem, and coming to an understanding of the lengths to which parents and families will go to solve such problems.

These were energetic discussions that revealed the vastness of their thinking and skills. In order to capture the essence of the discussions, I developed a Narrative Checklist (Figure 3.1) to use for whole-group or small-group discussions or with individual students for both oral and written work. In a group situation, the Yes/No column can be used to record the names of students who demonstrated particular skills. In any application, the checklist provided an efficient means to record information, highlight strengths, and identify weaknesses and areas for instruction. The checklist summary became invaluable, enabling me to focus on skills and individuals who needed opportunities and encouragement to probe the text.

Narrative Checklist

Name: Tom   Title of Text: Wild Cameron Women

Behaviours	Evidence	Yes/No	Comments
Attended to the text	• Focuses on the story depicted in the text • Disregards the illustrations • Understands the text • Keeps the discussion to the text	Yes Yes Yes Yes	Listened carefully
Engaged in the story	• Able to empathize with characters and/or the conflict • Relates story to own experience • Relates events within the story to each other	No No Yes	Made inferences Made connections, but didn't elaborate
Visualized the story	• Able to discuss and explain what they saw • Able to entertain individual visions • Able to explain their perspective	Yes Yes	Clearly explained
Divergent Thinking			
Substantiated thinking through references to the text	• Uses vocabulary from the text • Cites events or situations in the text • Explains and supports ideas with examples from the text	Yes Yes Yes	Noticed and reported detail
Took risks in expressing ideas	• States ideas without concern for peers' opinions or approval • States ideas and provides a rationale	Yes Yes	Clarified ideas
Interpreted and analyzed	• Develops ideas about the text • Provides thoughtful responses that explore the meaning of the text • Makes connections within and without the text	Yes Yes Yes	Made inferences Definitely interested in deeper meaning of Nana's role in solving the problem
Responses were lengthy and reflected probing for deeper meaning	• Questions author's construct • Speculates about the relationships between events • Understands story was a vehicle for presenting complex relationships • Able to clarify thinking and make ideas accessible to others	Yes Yes Yes Yes	Made inferences and connections Understood that text obscured what he understood Responded to Susan's question
Dialogue among Students			
	• Responds to another student's ideas with, e.g., "I agree… because…" "I also thought…" "I'm not sure that you're right because…" • Exchanges ideas • Accepts diversity in thinking • Interacts directly with each other	Yes Yes Yes	Followed up on Eve's statement about Nana

Figure 3.1B. The completed checklist reflects Tom's comments in the conversation reported above.

Many opportunities for this type of discussion preceded my shift to asking them for a written response to a text they had read independently. This was not going to be an easy leap. In preparation for this, we used the leads:

> I wondered…, I noticed…, I was confused…, I was surprised…,
>   I think that the author…, I felt…, I disliked…, I liked…, I could see
> the story happening…,

and collaborated on creating a written response that would serve as a model for them. The change to writing was, as expected, a formidable challenge. It is much easier to express oneself orally. Writing requires more skills in organizing thoughts, substantiating ideas, and dealing with grammar and spelling while expressing those thoughts and ideas. This time, they were working in isolation. They could neither respond to nor be inspired by a classmate's ideas. The difficulties this situation presented were evident in the range and quality of their written work. Writing proved to be something of a handicap for some students who struggled to achieve clarity and employ evidence to support their ideas. Their written answers did not do justice to the complexity of their thinking. However, there were some notable exceptions.

The following excerpt is taken from the notebook of a grade 2 boy who had read *Sadako and a Thousand Paper Cranes* (Coerr 1977). The story is of a real child, Sadako, who was living in Hiroshima, Japan, when the first atomic bomb was dropped on her city in August 1945 to end the Pacific phase of World War II. She later contracted leukemia from the radiation fallout and, in hospital, began folding one thousand paper cranes with the goal of having her wish to live granted. Although she died of the leukemia, her story continues to inspire other children.

> "I think that the author did a good job writing the book because just by telling me the story of one girl, it told how bad the atom bomb was."
>
> "I was confused because the United States decided to win the war with so much violence. I thought that the atom bomb was also bad because it killed lots of innocent people."

In these two responses, there is ample evidence that the student has reached out beyond the text to history and people. He has been able to generalize Sadako's story and to realize that she was just one person who died this way. He has demonstrated empathy and concern for people. More than that, he has questioned the moral integrity of a country at war and the parameters of war. He poses the questions: Who is the enemy? Is it a country's warriors or the entire population?

The student, in saying, "I wondered why in Japan, if a sick person folded 1,000 paper cranes, the gods would grant them a wish to be well again," is seeking an understanding of another culture's customs and beliefs. We understand his sense of disbelief as he questions what appears to be a simplistic and unscientific notion of how one preserves life. In saying, "I felt good for Sadako's friends because they finished the thousand paper cranes, and built a statue of her," he recognizes how the process of making cranes occupied everyone and helped them come to terms with her death.

His answers reflect his ability to contemplate and probe and to use written language to articulate his thoughts. There is much that he wants answered beyond the text. Most importantly, he has taken nothing at face value. His unusual skills were beyond those of most of his classmates.

This naturally meant that more experience, effort, modelling, and collaborating were needed to bridge the gap between the students' oral and written responses. Despite their struggles with the written component, I knew that this approach to reading stimulated their thinking. Not only did they make connections, within and without the text, and find implied meanings but they also engaged in a process that ultimately led to analysis and synthesis. They were actively using readers' strategies to comprehend, interpret, and probe the meaning of the text. Once mastered and regularly used, these metacognitive skills could be applied everywhere.

Working with non-fiction digital texts

I wanted to see how my students applied their metacognitive skills when reading websites. I began by introducing them to CG Kids Atlas on the Internet. This is a versatile website that provides information about Canada for children from grade one through high school. They can read, watch videos, look at maps, play games related to the selected topic, get fast facts, and pursue what interests them. Teachers can also find lesson plans by topic and grade.

This activity was a two-fold shift, from books to screen and from fiction to nonfiction. All the children were comfortable using computers and exploring websites, but had no prior exposure to this website. After allowing them time to explore the website, I used the same leads: I wondered…, I noticed…, I was confused…, I was surprised…, I think that the author…, I felt…, I disliked…, I liked…, as I had with stories.

They yielded some interesting responses, but little to no discussion. The children credited the website with presenting lots of information in a variety of different forms. However, the leads did not seem precise enough to garner deeper thoughts and dialogue. Apparently the leads needed rethinking. As a result I prepared five questions:

1. Why did they make this website?
2. Why did they include everything they did?
3. How is this website different from or the same as others that you look at?
4. Would you recommend it or not recommend it to others, and why?
5. How should people use this website?

Although these questions are more specific than the leads, they are open-ended and were not specific to this website. Consequently, they generated much discussion and interaction among the students, as the following comments show:

- Ruth told us that it provided people with interesting information about Canada.
  "I could learn about bears."
- Ken said that it divided information into topics.
  "You pick what you want to find out about."
- Ken added that it offered a variety of presentation formats.
  "You can do word searches or look at a video."
- Marjorie was excited that it invited readers to come back because there was lots to do.
  "We needed more time."
- Joanna appreciated the fact that it was not a "sticky" website because it did not use advertising and other devices to get you to come back.
  "It's a good website because it doesn't advertise anything. You go back to it because it's interesting, not to buy something."
- Ken liked what and how he could learn because it had word searches that other websites don't.
  "The word searches were fun and you learned to spell words."
- Joanna understood that it was intended for people who like to learn, but not for people who just want games.
  "Some people just like to play games, but don't want to learn anything. This wouldn't be good for them."
- Joanna recognized that it was good for both boys and girls who enjoy games, although she noted that more boys than girls tend to like to play games on websites.
  "Well, I think boys usually like websites that have games. Some girls like games too. So I'd say that it's good for both boys and girls."
- Ruth told us that it was useful for students, teachers, and adults.
  "There's so much information that it's good for everybody."
- Ruth also added that it provided information for research and for projects.
  "We could use it for projects and research."
- Marjorie realized that it was good for teaching and learning.
  "It teaches you lots. You can learn a lot."

What did their responses tell me about this process? Were the discussions and outcomes evidence of metacognitive reading skills? Once again, I developed a checklist, which can be used for whole-group or small-group discussions, or with individual students for both oral and written work. It provides an efficient means to record information, highlight strengths, and identify weaknesses and areas for instruction. This was invaluable for me. It confirmed that the students were indeed using some or all of the metacognitive skills, and it enabled me to focus on skills and individuals who needed opportunities and encouragement to navigate the website and probe the content.

Checklist—Reading and Making Meaning of Websites

Name: Joanna   Title of Text: CG Kids Atlas

Behaviours	Evidence	Yes/No	Comments
Navigate the website	• Able to find what he/she wanted • Uses icons • Understands website features • Moves around the website	Yes Yes Yes Yes	Found many components throughout
Follow instructions	• Able to interpret text and symbols to access features and areas of website • Able to understand and apply instructions	Yes Yes	Ditto
Understand, Use, and Discuss Website Content			
Extract, discuss and interpret information	• Understands website content • Able to discuss and explain content • Uses website language • Explains and supports ideas with examples from the website • Suggests how he/she could use this information	Yes Yes Yes Yes	
Make connections	• Makes connections without the website, e.g., to books, personal experience, videos. • Makes connections within the website • Explains and supports ideas with examples from the website	Yes Yes	Gender comments When asked
Took risks in expressing ideas	• States ideas without concern for peers' opinions or approval • States ideas and provides a rationale	Yes Yes	Confident
Interpreted and analyzed	• Develops ideas about the content • Provides thoughtful responses that explore the meaning of the content • Makes connections within and without the website	Yes Yes	Clearly and thoughtfully stated Connects to experience
Merits and Application of Website			
Identified features of the website	• Notes the variety of topics/subtopics on website • Notes whether website was sticky (games, gimmicks that draw you back) or not • Identifies commercial or non-commercial aspects	Yes Yes Yes	Very clear about this

Figure 3.2B. The completed checklist reflects Joanna's comments in the conversation reported above.

Gender differences	• Discusses and explains gender preferences for websites • Explains who would prefer to use the website and how they might use it	Yes Yes	Carefully stated
Evaluation of website and suggested uses	• Discusses what and how they learn from website • Determines the personal value • Suggests who is the expected audience	Yes Yes Yes	Values what she can learn Broad audience
Dialogue Among Students			
Listened to each other	• Responds to another student's ideas with, e.g., "I agree… because…" "I also thought…" "I'm not sure that you're right because…" • Exchanges ideas • Accepts diversity in thinking • Interacts directly with each other	Yes	Stated ideas in response to others, more summary statements than interactive

Figure 3.2B. (cont'd)

Despite their success, it was apparent that the students needed many more opportunities to enhance their ability to employ metacognition. To facilitate this, I told them that I wanted to learn about geckos and projected a website on a screen. As with *Wild Cameron Women*, I shared my thinking as I explored the website. On another day, I told them that I wanted to learn about kangaroos. I showed them how to have two websites open simultaneously and how to move back and forth between them to find and clarify information, and support their metacognitive thinking. Once again, I invited them in with "What are your thoughts?"

On a third occasion, I repeated the above procedure with the addition of Microsoft Word, the word-processing program, although any word-processing program on your computer would serve the same purpose. I was able to demonstrate how to make jot notes, record our thinking, and keep track of information or questions that arose as we looked at the websites. This process added another tool to the metacognitive kit bag. Now all they needed was time and the opportunity to apply these skills. Our course was set.

Fostering metacognition when using all texts

Students who read using metacognition are more deeply engaged and go deeper into the text. They need to apply these skills on a regular basis. In my classroom, I have a card with a list of leads on it. Beside it, there is a pad of small sticky notes. While the children are reading, they use the notes. They write a lead or their thoughts on a note and stick it on the text that triggered their thinking. The notes are substitutes for the highlighters or margin notes that students and adults employ in the books they own. Just like adults, the children return to their notes to jog their memories about their thoughts while they are writing or discussing the text. I have often watched students line up the sticky notes on desktops or notebooks, rearranging them until they have found a satisfactory way to organize their response. They persisted in reviewing and rethinking the meanings and determining ways to present them in writing.

Now I had come full circle in my exploration of how to integrate instruction in both traditional and new literacies. My search had answered my own questions and simultaneously confirmed Donald Leu's statement that foundational reading skills must precede new literacies. But how do we ensure that this is happening, or will happen, in classrooms?

I strongly advocate that teachers give priority to text printed in books in the early stages of reading development. There is nothing more precious or valuable to a child than turning the pages of a book, returning to loved pages, pointing fingers at words, moving a finger under a line of text, seeing the spaces between words, sharing the book with a friend, or tucking it under an arm when walking down the hall. These encounters are personal and stand as markers in a reader's progress. Yet some would view these as sentimental acts. Perhaps that is a valid viewpoint, but the amount of time spent with books and print is important in creating readers, and we must accompany them in that pursuit, providing guidance and instruction in all the intricacies of reading.

At the same time, we must ensure that our students have ample opportunity to explore the world of new literacies. Then they will delve deeper, unearth meaning, read critically, and assess the value of these sources. Our guidance is critical to their success in deciphering the worlds of writing.

Undoubtedly, there are many ways to foster metacognition. However, I believe it is formal instruction in, and the application of, metacognition that leads students to ask questions of themselves and to think about the text and its relationship to the world and to themselves, and that induces them to read in the most meaningful way. Only then can we be sure that we are providing them with the learning opportunity to experience text in all its myriad forms.

REFERENCES

Coerr, Eleanor. 1977. *Sadako and the thousand paper cranes*, New York: Bantam Doubleday.

Henry, Laurie A. 2006. SEARCHing for an answer: The critical role of new literacies while reading on the internet, *The Reading Teacher*, 59.7, 614–627.

Hull, Maureen and Judith C. Mills. 2000. *Wild Cameron Women*. Toronto, ON: Stoddart Kids.

Leu, Donald J., Charles K. Kinzer, Julie L. Coiro, and David W. Cammack. 2004. "Toward a theory of new literacies emerging from the internet and other information and communication technologies." In R. B. Ruddell and N. Unrau, N. (Eds.). *Theoretical Models and Processes of Reading*. (1570–1613). Newark, DE: International Reading Association.

Pressley, Michael. 2002. "Metacognition and self-regulated comprehension." In A. E. Farstrup, and S. Samuels (Eds.), *What Research Has to Say About Reading Instruction* (291–309). Newark, DE: International Reading Association.

Sutherland-Smith, Wendy. 2002. "Weaving the literacy web: Changes in reading from page to screen." *The Reading Teacher*, 55.7, 662–669.

RESOURCES

How to select websites
- Determine your teaching and learning objectives before you look for a website.
- Avoid sites that are commercially funded and filled with advertisements, or those that solicit funds.
- Look for topics of educational value that relate to curriculum areas or are of interest to students.
- To ensure that a website meets your personal criteria, check it ahead of class, even if it was recommended by colleagues or students.
- Look for sites that allow for divergent thinking, encourage connections, and invite dialogue.
- Look for sites that offer varied presentation modes to allow for the range of skills in your class.
- Review the sites recommended by your school library and board.

Websites for children (accessed March 27, 2009)

CG Kids Atlas, Canadian Geographic Online: <http://www.canadiangeographic.ca/cgkidsatlas/default_en.asp>

Enchanted Learning: <http://www.enchantedlearning.com/Home.html>

Our animals: <www.abc.net.au/schoolstv/animals/KANGAROOS.htm>

Kids' Planet: <www.kidsplanet.org/factsheets/kangaroo.html>

Ask Kids: <http://www.askkids.com>

KidsClick: <http://www.kidsclick.org>

Yahoo! Kids: <http://kids.yahoo.com>

Kids Planet: <http://www.kidsplanet.org/factsheets/kangaroo.html>

National Geographic: <http://animals.nationalgeographic.com>

Library and Archives Canada: <http://www.collectionscanada.gc.ca>

KidSpace @ The Internet Public Library: <http://www.ipl.org/div/kidspace>

Narrative Checklist

Name: _____ Title of Text: _____

Behaviours	Evidence	Yes/No	Comments
Attended to the text	• Focuses on the story depicted in the text • Disregards the illustrations • Understands the text • Keeps the discussion to the text		
Engaged in the story	• Able to empathize with characters and/or the conflict • Relates story to own experience • Relates events within the story to each other		
Visualized the story	• Able to discuss and explain what they saw • Able to entertain individual visions • Able to explain their perspective		
Divergent Thinking			
Substantiated thinking through references to the text	• Uses vocabulary from the text • Cites events or situations in the text • Explains and supports ideas with examples from the text		
Took risks in expressing ideas	• States ideas without concern for peers' opinions or approval • States ideas and provides a rationale		
Interpreted and analyzed	• Develops ideas about the text • Provides thoughtful responses that explore the meaning of the text • Makes connections within and without the text		
Responses were lengthy and reflected probing for deeper meaning	• Questions author's construct • Speculates about the relationships between events • Understands story was a vehicle for presenting complex relationships • Able to clarify thinking and make ideas accessible to others		
Dialogue among Students			
	• Responds to another student's ideas with, e.g., "I agree… because…" "I also thought…" "I'm not sure that you're right because…" • Exchanges ideas • Accepts diversity in thinking • Interacts directly with each other		

Figure 3.1A.

Checklist—Reading and Making Meaning of Websites

Name: _____ Title of Text: _____

Behaviours	Evidence	Yes/No	Comments
Navigate the website	• Able to find what he/she wanted • Uses icons • Understands website features • Moves around the website		
Follow instructions	• Able to interpret text and symbols to access features and areas of website • Able to understand and apply instructions		
Understand, Use, and Discuss Website Content			
Extract, discuss and interpret information	• Understands website content • Able to discuss and explain content • Uses website language • Explains and supports ideas with examples from the website • Suggests how he/she could use this information		
Make connections	• Makes connections without the website, e.g., to books, personal experience, videos. • Makes connections within the website • Explains and supports ideas with examples from the website		
Took risks in expressing ideas	• States ideas without concern for peers' opinions or approval • States ideas and provides a rationale		
Interpreted and analyzed	• Develops ideas about the content • Provides thoughtful responses that explore the meaning of the content • Makes connections within and without the website		
Merits and Application of Website			
Identified features of the website	• Notes the variety of topics/subtopics on website • Notes whether website was sticky (games, gimmicks that draw you back) or not • Identifies commercial or non-commercial aspects		

Figure 3.2A.

Gender differences	• Discusses and explains gender preferences for websites • Explains who would prefer to use the website and how they might use it		
Evaluation of website and suggested uses	• Discusses what and how they learn from website • Determines the personal value • Suggests who is the expected audience		
Dialogue among Students			
Listened to each other	• Responds to another student's ideas with, e.g., "I agree… because…" "I also thought…" "I'm not sure that you're right because…" • Exchanges ideas • Accepts diversity in thinking • Interacts directly with each other		

Figure 3.2A. (cont'd)

Chapter 4

Power Up Picture Books
Kristin Main

Once upon a time, there was a classroom without a computer...

There were no computers in the classroom when I started school. The need for information meant a trip to the library and a perusal of the card catalogue. There was something very fulfilling about the whole experience. I remember rummaging through the yellowed index cards and eagerly racing to the stacks, anticipation high. Would the book be there?

Now, I go online. I type a few words into my favourite search engine and, within seconds, a copy of the desired text or the location of the nearest copy accompanied by a status report of its availability appears on screen. I collect mostly electronic files now—PDF for my favourite articles, MP3 for audio books, and JPG for illustrations. Technology is now embedded in my daily literacy. But still, there is something about having a copy of a book. There is a tangible relationship formed between the reader and the text. And this is where I am torn. Technology fascinates me, but I will always love my books. My love of both types of text has guided me in my quest to "power up" books and to integrate technology into my literacy program, specifically into my "read-alouds" with my adolescent students.

The term *power up* is taken from computer games. It means that a participant in a computer game collects predetermined objects over the course of a game and receives an instant advantage—usually added power or extended play. This got me thinking about books in the classroom. How could I power up picture books to extend my students' understanding of the books? Was there a way to draw on the digital experiences of my students? How could I preserve the integrity of the read-aloud and enhance the experience through technology?

The read-aloud

I remember the first time I read a picture book to one of my older classes. I was nervous. It was bound to be either a tremendous success or a miserable failure. But I had carefully selected my book following Osborn's (2001) guidelines for selecting picture books for young adults. She recommends picture books that include

- mature themes
- complex illustrations
- more difficult text
- subtle meanings
- multiple layers of meaning
- use of fiction and nonfiction texts

> **READ-ALOUD TIPS**
>
> Adapted from *The Read-Aloud Handbook* (Jim Trelease, 2006)
> - Prepare students for read-alouds by creating an inviting listening environment.
> - Begin by introducing the author, illustrator, and title. Remember that the work was created by people. Help the students connect with the people behind the work.
> - Use the cover to encourage the students to make predictions based on the illustration and title.
> - While reading, use expressive voices and allow time for students to hear and consider the words. This means read slowly!
> - Allow the students to doodle while you read to keep their hands busy while they listen.
> - Select books that you enjoy so your enthusiasm will transfer.
> - Ensure you have enough time to stimulate the students with the read-aloud, not frustrate them by getting cut off too soon.
> - Let the students' interpretations, rather than your own, be the focus of follow-up discussions.

And so I began with the familiar opening to *Where the wild things are* (Sendak 1963): "The night Max wore his wolf suit and made mischief of one kind..." and followed the recommendations of Jim Trelease (2006, see above).

The discussion that followed filled the entire class period. Some students made text-to-self connections through memories of hearing the story as young children; others made text-to-text connections with other familiar childhood stories. They spoke about the parent–child relationships and what unconditional love means. They spoke of the illustrations and the use of colour. They identified and some even empathized with the emotional nature of Max's journey. They even talked about how different they believed the story would be if Max were a girl.

This read-aloud worked for many different reasons, beginning with the fact that my grade 7 students connected with the story. It was a safe medium for them to consider mature themes. Bloem and Padak (1996) point out that people of all ages enjoy and can become engrossed in a story being read to them. Actually, "Stories can be powerful. It is not just the children who can feel that power and lose themselves to another world" (49).

The characters' expressions helped students, especially males, develop their awareness of the role that facial expressions and emotions play in moving from a concrete understanding to a more abstract level (Zambo, 2007). Students "gain a deeper sensitivity to the characters' emotions and intentions, and greater insight into the issues and struggles portrayed in the books, than may be possible when reading the text alone." In fact, this process can "enhance their understanding of even the most complex social issues when reading picture books" (Burke and Stagg Peterson 2007, 74).

The read-aloud itself addressed the needs and interests of my adolescent male readers by meeting one of the basic needs identified by Zambo (2007)—that is, creating a positive classroom environment for working with picture books. Because the introduction to picture books was initiated by me and the responsibility for text selection was not theirs, the boys in the class were freer to interact with the text.

The read-aloud had been a success with my students. But I kept thinking about the technological nature of my students' day-to-day literacies. I wondered what would happen if I powered up this process, if I drew from the students' technological strengths and integrated them with the read-aloud.

I was looking for ways to create what McVee and her colleagues (2008) call "computer-mediated epiphanies" where students use their familiarity with technology, such as the computer, as a tool with which to unpack literacy (446). I decided to merge a traditional read-aloud with picture books into a digital format to draw from the students' digital worlds while honouring the printed text.

The digital connection

One of my favourite picture books to work with is *Stanley's Party* (Bailey 2003), illustrated by Bill Slavin. Stanley is a lovable dog who is left alone in the house often enough that temptation sets in and he begins to break rules. He is faced with many complex issues, especially for a dog, about trust, respect, empathy, integrity, and responsibility.

Students can use critical literacy to read both the print and the illustrations. *Stanley's Party* provides them with accessible, relevant content that can be discussed in greater depth to align more closely with their levels of maturity. Students have much to consider when reading the illustrations because of the wonderful detail, especially the expressive nature of the dogs.

In the past, when I have used a read-aloud format, I have circulated the classroom as I read the text to show students the pictures. With most picture books, there is much for the students to absorb. Specific to *Stanley's Party*, the students need to be able to make connections between the inner dialogue, from the canine's perspective, and the dynamic between the human characters and their expectations and behaviour. Between reacting to the text and trying to see the pictures, the students never seemed to get enough of Stanley. Because of this, I decided to use slide show presentation software to show the illustrations while reading and talking about the book.

The technical how-to

Slide show presentation software (e.g., Microsoft PowerPoint 2007) is one of the most readily available means of integrating technology into the read-aloud experience, but you also need a digital scanner and an LCD projector—the digital scanner to make a copy of the text, the easy-to-use format of PowerPoint to organize the copies, and the LCD projector to display the images on a screen.

There are several stages in powering up the picture book. First, you have to scan the selected pages (keep in mind, for copyright considerations, the copied portion cannot exceed 10 percent of the work) and save them as a PDF (portable document format) file, that is, as digital copies. Next, you use screen capture software to take a picture of each image. It is possible to work with the PDF files directly, but if you accidentally include page edges or fingers during the scanning process, you can use the screen capture software to select the portion of the image that provides more clearly defined lines.

At this stage, the images are ready to prepare for presentation. Although you can just project the PDF images of the pages on to the screen or use any software program that is compatible with PDF files, I prefer using slide show presentation software because it allows me to flip back and forth easily between images. Another advantage is that you can apply pre-set layouts to the slides. By selecting a layout that has space for multiple inserts, such as a title and content, you can include the illustration and the corresponding text on the same slide. Using slide show presentation software along with the LCD projector, you can juxtapose other text or images with the originals in the picture book.

For classroom discussions, slide show presentation software such as Microsoft PowerPoint 2007 offers you several options. By right-clicking on the mouse, you can direct the pointer arrow to parts of an image, for example, a subtle look in the eye of an illustrated character. Another option is the choice of different pens and highlighters that you can control with the mouse. They are especially useful for highlighting text or for free-hand design to isolate a specific aspect of the text or illustrations. If your computer has touch-screen capacity, then you can write or print questions on the screen as the class dialogue progresses, which gives your students the opportunity to shape the flow of discussion.

Other features of slide show presentation software that can enhance the reading experience draw from the characteristics of a big book. You can animate the presentation by selecting different effects as the slides play. I usually select the one that most closely imitates the turning of pages. The animation features also apply to the timing—you can choose to have the slides advance automatically and predetermine an amount of time for the class to work with one particular slide. Or, you can cue the groups to move their discussion on to the next topic; I like to advance the slides myself because I can allow unlimited time for class discussion. Another animation tool lets you use a sound effect as the slides advance. All animation features provide the option of applying your settings to all the slides, which can save you time; without that option, you would have to select all the animations one by one for each slide.

Once you have completed your slide show, you can present it through an LCD projector. Some LCD projectors are fitted with a document camera, that is, a video camera attached to the projector. With this attachment, you can slide the picture book under the video camera and project the image onto the screen.

The application

To work with my students on critical literacy using *Stanley's Party*, I focused on one page from the beginning of the story and two pages toward the end of the story. I created a slideshow organized into four slides, using only three pages of the original picture book.

Slide 1
The first slide is the illustration of Stanley, which also appears on the following 3 slides. I ask the students to consider the picture and share their impressions with their neighbour.

Slide 2
I then show the same image of Stanley with the following discussion questions to guide critical literacy:
- What emotion is Stanley feeling?
  - How do you know this?
- What does Stanley think about his owners?
  - Why do you believe this?
- Who holds the most power in this illustration?
  - What features of the illustration support this?

Slide 3

Then I show the third slide—the illustration accompanied by the text.

I list the same questions underneath the illustration and text, with the addition of one more. I ask students to consider both the illustration and the text.

- What emotion is Stanley feeling?
  - How do you know this?
- Who holds the most power in this illustration?
  - What features of the illustration support this?
- What does Stanley think about his owners?
  - Why do you believe this?
- What is the effect of connecting the illustration to the text?
  - Have you revised any of your previous responses?

Figure 4.1.

Figure 4.2. Text reads: All the dogs except Stanley had to go home. Stanley helped his people clean up. It took two whole days.

Slide 4

The fourth slide I use juxtaposes Stanley before and after he gets caught breaking the rules by his people.

The discussion that accompanies this slide revisits the previous questions. I ask students to support their answers to the following questions with references to both the text and the illustrations:

- How have Stanley's emotions changed?
- How do you think his future actions will change?
- How has Stanley's relationship with his people changed?
- What message do you think that the author of this story, Linda Bailey, and the illustrator, Bill Slavin, are trying to convey?

After this, I move into the focus topic and continue with a reflective journal, writing assignment, and small-group discussions or role-playing. Depending on the grade and maturity of the students, the possible topics for extension include respect, empathy, communication, trust, and issues such as animal advocacy. Students need time to draw connections between the text and their own lives, including the world around them, in order to solidify learning. I often leave the last slide on the projector as the students continue their assignment so that they may look again at the text and illustrations on the screen, which is another advantage of the technology—the entire class can work with the same text.

Students do the powering up

In my work using the powered-up picture books with the students, it quickly became clear that if my intent was to draw from the students' technological literacies, then they should be the producers as well as the consumers of the digital texts. Here are some ideas for engaging students in producing their own powered-up picture book presentations:

Student Task and Technology Involved

Student Task	What Technology This Involves

Text-to-Self Connection
• Scan a page from a picture book that demonstrates a character reacting to a challenging situation.
• Include the text.
• Critique the character's reaction and share a range of positive options including what you would do if you were faced with the same situation.
	• scanning images
	
	• using slideshow presentation software to:
	  – create a slide that uses a comparison format
	  – place a visual beside a text list

Text-to-Text Connection
• Scan a page from a picture book that focuses on a character's emotional reaction to a situation.
• Scan a page from a second picture book that demonstrates another character's emotional reaction to a similar situation.
• Compare the characters' reactions. Consider how they would have reacted in the other situation.
	• scanning images
	• using slideshow presentation software to:
	  – create a slide that uses a comparison format by placing a visual beside a visual
	  – use a visual pointer tool to identify the emotion expressed (may include specific aspects of a facial expression or body language)
	  – create a text slide to highlight key information

Text-to-World Connection
• Scan a page from your favourite picture book and juxtapose the image next to an image that represents a current social issue.
• Explain the connections between the image and the issue.
	• scanning images
	• using slideshow presentation software to:
	  – create a slide that uses a comparison format
	  – create a text slide to highlight key information

Figure 4.3.

Our students are bombarded by an ever-increasing variety of text and technology. The concept of powering up picture books allows students to draw from their multimodal natures and explore books in a manner that the printed pages alone do not allow. These pages do, however, invite students to draw from their own lives and their own technological abilities as the story and illustrations provide the opportunity to address topical issues. Because the students are not overwhelmed by weighty text, they can immerse themselves in the content and concentrate on constructing their understandings and interpretations in the medium of their choice, whether it's the creation of a slideshow, a blog, a digital movie, or a webcast. Just as we teachers are creating space for newer technologies and technological literacies, we need to remember that picture books still hold a space in the students' literacy experiences. By powering up picture books, we are helping students extend their awareness of picture books and yet also honouring the students' digital knowledge and experiences.

CONSIDERATIONS: PUBLIC DOMAIN AND COPYRIGHT PROTECTED WORKS

In addition to using parts of picture books, you may use public domain works. These are works that are not protected by copyright and can be used in any manner, for any purpose, by anyone. Public domain work includes print and audio files of novels, picture books, fairy tales, fables, nursery rhymes, illustrations, and even music. The easiest way to locate public domain works is to conduct an Internet search with the key term "public domain." It is important for students to understand the difference between public domain work and copyright-protected work.

In powering up picture books, it's important to think about those who created the works. Authors and illustrators in conjunction with numerous others create the characters and stories that stimulate our children's imaginations and inspire their creativity while providing a forum to foster critical literacy skills. This means that we need to respect copyright laws.

The definition of copying, according to Access Copyright, includes such common processes as creating copies through photocopying, typing and word processing, making overheads or slides, or tracing. The amount that teachers are allowed to copy (as covered by a school licence) is up to 10 percent of a published work or the following, whichever is greater:

- an entire single short story, play, essay, or poem from a book or periodical containing other works
- an entire article from a newspaper, magazine, or journal
- an entire entry from a reference work (encyclopaedia, dictionary)
- an entire reproduction of an artistic work from a publication containing other works
- a whole chapter from a book, as long as that chapter does not comprise more than 20 percent of the book

This means that in order for a teacher to copy a complete story it would have to be included in an anthology. The majority of my picture book collection is individual books, which means that I am only able to copy 10 percent of these works. However, I quickly discovered that it is absolutely amazing how much can be done with 10 percent of a great book.

REFERENCES

Bailey, Linda. 2003. *Stanley's Party*. Bill Slavin, illus. Toronto, ON: Kids Can Press.

Bloem, Patricia L. and Nancy D. Padak. 1996. Picture books, young adult books, and adult literacy learners. *Journal of Adolescent & Adult Literacy,* 40 (1), 48-53.

Burke, Ann and Shelley Stagg Peterson. 2007. "A multidisciplinary approach to literacy through picture books and drama." *English Journal,* 96 (3), 74–78.

Canadian Copyright Licensing Agency. *Access Copyright.* <http://www.accesscopyright.ca/Default.aspx> (accessed March 27, 2009).

McVee, Mary, Nancy Bailey, and Lynn Shanahan. 2008. "Technology lite: Advice and reflections for the technologically unsavvy." *Journal of adolescent and adult literacy,* 51 (6), 444-448.

Osborn, Sunya. 2001. Picture books for young adult readers. ALAN Review, 28 (3), 24–26. <http://scholar.lib.vt.edu/ejournals/ALAN/v28n3/osborn.html> (accessed March 27, 2009).

Sendak, Maurice. 1963. *Where the wild things are.* New York, NY: HarperCollins.

Trelease, Jim. 2006. *The read-aloud handbook.* New York, NY: Penguin Books. <http://www.trelease-on-reading.com/rah-ch4.html> (accessed March 27, 2009).

Zambo, Debby. 2007. "Using picture books to provide archetypes to young boys: Extending the ideas of William Brozo." *The Reading Teacher,* 61 (2), 124–131

Chapter 5

Scaffolding Early Literacy Using the SMART Board

Brenda Stein Dzaldov and Elana Shapiro Davidson

The SMART Board, an interactive whiteboard, can be used for assessment and instruction. It is a place for collaborative learning communities to work, and it provides oral language practice and opportunities to scaffold all areas of literacy instruction. The SMART Board is capable of giving specific, timely, and accurate feedback to learners as they interact with this technological tool. The SMART Board allows teachers to incorporate digital text into their everyday teaching in a meaningful way and, best of all, it is engaging and fun! Our experiences with the SMART Board in early literacy instruction are born out of good teaching. Anything that an excellent teacher would normally do can be done even better using a SMART Board.

The installation of SMART Boards in our primary classrooms has completely altered our way of planning lessons in all content areas. In this chapter, we focus on ideas for using the SMART Board as a teaching tool within the framework of a balanced literacy program. If teachers have basic knowledge of technology and are provided with a demonstration of using the toolbars and the gallery, the SMART Board can become a very teacher-friendly tool with endless possibilities for enhancing instruction and using digital text meaningfully. In our classroom, we have seen that students are motivated to participate in literacy activities because the SMART Board has added an element of fun, engagement, and excitement to their learning. The SMART Board can accommodate and support a variety of different modalities. It is an interactive tool that incorporates sound, video, images, and print—therefore, you can plan lessons to address more than one modality at a time. In addition, the SMART Board is large enough for a number of students to interact and work together, which encourages conversation, problem solving, and collaboration—which all support literacy learning.

THE BASICS

Before creating your SMART Board lesson, take some time to familiarize yourself with all the tools of the technology. In other words, you need to play a little. You can load the SMART Board software onto your home computer and explore the technology at home. The only drawback is that you have to use your mouse instead of the interactive, touch-screen whiteboard. With the whiteboard, you can use your finger or SMART Board pen instead of the mouse to control all computer applications and operations.

Toolbars

The two tool areas that are highly useful are shown below. You will use them when planning the lesson, while the lesson is in progress, and when the students are using the SMART Board independently.

Figure 5.1.

Top Toolbar

Many of the tools at the top of the SMART Board screen are familiar tools from any word-processing program. When you hover your mouse over an icon, an explanation appears.

Open: For example, if you click on this icon, a FULL SCREEN will appear.

Undo: This tool will visibly remove all icons at the top, side, and bottom of your screen to maximize the viewing area.

Side Screen Toolbar

The **Page Sorter** allows you to change the page on your SMART Board screen. If your lesson has more than one page, use your finger to tap on the page you want, and it will appear on the interactive, whiteboard screen.

The **Gallery** contains a collection of ready-made lessons from which you can choose. You have the option of selecting your country, your grade level, and curriculum area. The lessons you find can be modified to meet your students' needs. In addition, the gallery contains clip art, videos, and interactive tools that you can insert into any lesson. The attachment feature will save any attachments that you import such as picture, music, or sound files.

Note: It is useful to configure your computer to notify you about the availability of upgrade packages for SMART Board software. The screen-captures shown here are based on Version 9.7 of the program.

Figure 5.2.

Where to begin

It can be overwhelming when you are first planning how to integrate the SMART Board into your daily literacy program. We will begin with a simple, yet effective, daily shared-reading lesson that you probably already do with your students—a Morning Message. If you begin every morning with a Morning Message that incorporates such elements as high frequency sight words, practising phonological awareness skills and phonics activities, and introducing new vocabulary, you'll find that using the SMART Board can elevate your students' learning experience to a whole new level.

The Morning Message (Figure 5.3) is one that the students read as a shared experience. By dragging any shape with the touch of a finger, you can move that shape anywhere on the screen. The students may eagerly anticipate that you have covered some words in order to have them predict what word is hiding underneath. They may need to do a "think, pair, and share" in which the teacher tells the students to take a minute or two and think about the question, pair with a partner for a short discussion, and finally share their ideas with the whole group (Kagan 1994) in order to predict the words that are hiding. The students consistently display great excitement in what they feel is a game. You can move the shape slowly, revealing only one letter at a time. If they see that the word begins (or ends) with a different letter than they had thought, they may need to return to their small groups to further discuss what word may be hiding.

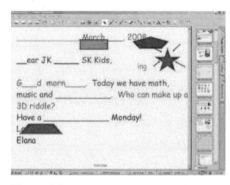

Figure 5.3.

You can divide words into parts and have students reconnect them by dragging the parts back together. We do this with letter clusters, such as searching for the *oo* in "Good morning" or for prefixes and suffixes. Children are able to move the text—everything on the SMART Board can be erased, saved, and reset—and this can be done by each child at some point during the day. All children learn from activities like mixing up the words in a sentence and putting them back together.

After reading the Morning Message, you can further extend your students' knowledge in many ways. The SMART Board allows you to insert a link to any source by touching an image or text on your screen. By using the **Insert Link** function, you or your students can tap on an image or text and be linked to another screen that you have created or to a website of your choice. Our students benefit from playing collaboratively on interactive websites (Figure 5.4) that focus on a range of literacy skills, including phonological awareness activities, alphabet activities, and independent reading and writing activities.

Figure 5.4. Starfall: <www.starfall.com> a free website that focuses on literacy.

With the SMART Board, timely and accurate feedback can be provided to students while the teacher is working elsewhere in the classroom. In Figure 5.5, a JK student is playing a word game that the teacher previously modelled and that two children are now working on

Figure 5.5.

independently. The task is to drag the appropriate letter into a box with a corresponding picture. If they forget a letter sound, they do not need to ask a teacher. Instead, they can tap on the letter to hear the sound. The program will allow them to drop only the correct letter into the box. When they get it right, the word changes and allows them to move to a new word. In addition, the SMART Board lends itself well to creating conversational communities. The students are collaborating on the task and discussing how to solve the problem together.

Shared, interactive, and independent writing

Figure 5.6.

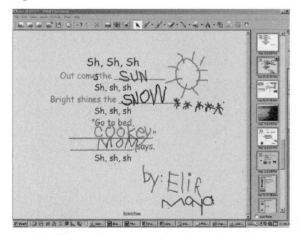

Figure 5.7.

The Morning Message activity can easily become a shared or interactive writing experience by leaving some of the message blank. All shared interactive writing experiences (messages, lists, charts, and stories) that have previously been done on chart paper can be composed on the SMART board with your class. Your students can also interact with the text, using their fingers or using one of the digital pens at the bottom of the screen.

After having shared an interactive writing experience with this Morning Message, students independently came in pairs to the SMART Board to rewrite parts of the message. They were able to save the message to share with their peers afterward before a new pair of students began working

After working with this poem many times, the students worked in groups to rewrite parts of the poem. Before the students worked on this independently, we first met as a group to reflect on the poem and give students a chance to discuss possible alternative words that would make sense in the context of this poem.

It is important to debug the text genre for students before introducing fiction or nonfiction texts on the SMART Board, in the same way that you debug any text form when you introduce it.

Reading aloud, shared reading, and independent reading

The SMART Board provides our students with the chance to listen to stories being read to them by many different story readers with text highlighted as it is read, and to watch video that accompanies the text. This takes the place of our listening centre because the students can interact with the text. While a book is being read to them, they have the opportunity to pause it, find and circle words that they recognize, add to the illustrations, and save and print the story to take home. They are able to follow along the highlighted text with their fingers and rewind and listen to a page again. There are a variety of sources on the Internet available to provide this opportunity for your students.

Once you have finished *reading* the story *aloud* and the students are familiar with the text, it may become a *shared reading* experience for a teacher with a few students. The shared reading experience can ultimately turn into an *independent reading* experience. In our class, the students were excited to listen to some of their favourite stories on the SMART Board more than once. We found that, as teachers, we could continue working with small groups of students in other areas of the classroom while the rest of the students could listen to a read-aloud from the SMART Board. However, if the teacher is not part of the read-aloud, the students can miss the prediction and reflection opportunities. You can prompt the students through your lesson on the SMART Board to share predictions either before the story begins or at certain points during the reading, as a collaborative activity. After the story, they can also share reflections orally with their peers or in a writing response on the SMART Board.

The SMART Board can enhance your read-alouds or author study units. In this example, the students have been studying books written by Robert Munsch and illustrated by Michael Martchenko. With proper scaffolding, the teacher can have the SMART Board play a role and allow the students to continue the study independently. In this picture, students are watching *50 Below Zero* (1986). By inserting a link to <www.Tumblebooks.com> (e-books for kids), the teacher can let the students **hear** the story being read to them, **watch** the text highlighted as the words are read, and **watch** movable illustrations. The children can pause the story or rewind to a page they may have missed. They can also pause the story to engage in a broad range of activities with the text, such as finding and circling high frequency words that they know, underlining spoken parts, and so on. One child can add to the illustrations, then just as easily erase it so that another child can do the same.

Figure 5.8.

Figure 5.9.

You can insert a photo of the author, in this case Robert Munsch, into your SMART Board lesson for the students. You can also insert a link directly onto the photo that, when clicked on, will take your students to an interview with Robert Munsch on YouTube <www.youtube.com>.

When your students have finished listening to all your chosen author's stories, have them use the SMART Board to respond to the stories through writing and art. Some authors have an extensive collection of literature and, when you ask children at the end of a unit which book was their favourite, you can remind them of all the books they have studied. You could put all the books in an "author's bucket" or write all the titles on chart paper. With the SMART Board, you could produce an image of each book cover for the students to review.

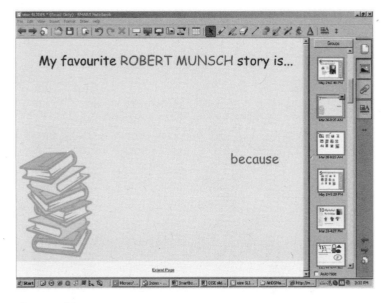

Figure 5.10.

This screen was created so that each student could write about their favourite Robert Munsch story. The sentence has been started for them. The students were able to rewrite the sentence starter, drag the *infinitely cloned* sentence and make it their own, or begin the response in their own way. The word *because* is a tricky word to spell, so it has been infinitely cloned so that each student can choose to drag the word into their sentence. By writing on the SMART Board with the digital pen, students can build their confidence as writers and be more willing to take risks because they can erase any of their attempts and try again.

Figure 5.11.

Section Two: *Engaging with Texts in Print and on Screen* 53

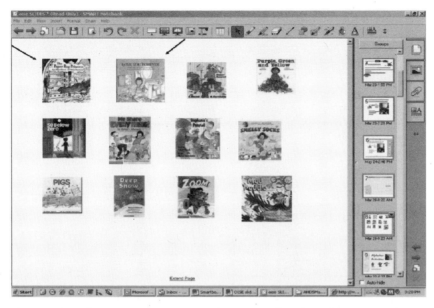

Figure 5.12. The INFINITE CLONER tool can reproduce any object or word an unlimited number of times.

Choral reading experiences on the SMART Board

Poetry and chants are an essential part of every successful balanced literacy program. In the past, teachers wrote all weekly poems on chart paper for the students to read, interpret, and respond to together. Afterwards, the teacher could have students practise the poem independently or manipulate the poem by mixing up the sentences or rewriting parts of the poem so students could make it their own. The poem by Sonja Dunn in the figure above is just one of the many poems that our students have interacted with on the SMART Board. We chose this poem in order to teach a variety of concepts—one was the phonemic blend "sh." In addition, some students were beginning to incorporate quotation marks into their writing.

After reading the poem, the students used the Page Sorter to go to the next screen, where they were presented with the challenge of putting the cut-up poem back in original sequence. The program was written so that an entire sentence could be dragged at one time. The lines were provided to help the students match sentence length to the lines. A feedback feature was provided, that is, students were taught how to use the Page Sorter so they could check whether they

Figure 5.13.

Figure 5.14.

Figure 5.15.

Figure 5.16.

correctly sequenced the poem instead of asking a teacher to "check their work."

Every time that a student tapped on "sh" they heard the sound that it makes. The picture depicts how their mouth must look when they make the sound. For this screen, students worked together to make sure that their partner had their lips and teeth in the position resembling the image on the SMART Board.

Once all children had done this, they proceeded to the next screen, which had a word game for them to play focusing on the "sh" sound <http://www.starfall.com/n/skills/sh/load/htm?f>.

After re-assembling this poem into the proper order, each student read it independently to a friend. Students who needed a reminder of how the poem sounded were able to tap on the title of the poem that linked to a video recording of another student reading the poem. This allowed all students to achieve success in reading and listening to the poem independently. The SMART Board allows you to insert any picture or video clip. This video clip was taken using a digital camera and then inserted into the lesson using the link feature.

Conclusion

With careful lesson planning, you will find that the SMART Board offers limitless possibilities for excellent early literacy instruction. It is important that you not use the SMART Board as just another worksheet or as just another way to display print text. Instead, try creating conversational communities where students interact with and support each other by coaching, requesting, rephrasing, attempting, and socially negotiating oral language.

As well, give careful consideration to how students will interact with the text. The SMART Board offers students the opportunity to interact with digital text and receive feedback. Giving students increased chances for independent practice of knowledge and skills is important, but the teacher must first model these for the students. When planning to use the SMART Board, capitalize on your students' different learning styles by giving them the opportunity to integrate their learning strengths—auditory skills, visual abilities, and kinesthetic experiences. Best of all, the SMART Board is an engaging form of teaching and learning that fosters an incredible enthusiasm among our young students.

REFERENCES

Dunn, Sonja. 1990. *Crackers and crumbs: Chants for whole language learning.* Markham, ON: Pembroke Publishers.

Kagan, Spencer. 1994. *Cooperative learning.* San Clemente, CA: Kagan Publishing.

Pressley, Michael. 2005. *Reading instruction that works: The case for balanced teaching*, 3rd ed. New York: Guilford Press.

Reeves, Douglas B. 2004. *Accountability in action: A blueprint for learning organizations*, 2nd ed. Denver, Colorado: Advanced Learning Press.

Swartz, Larry et al. 2001. *Crackers and crumbs: Rhymes, rhythms, and patterns for language learning.* Toronto: Lingo Media.

RESOURCES

Websites

NB: It is essential that you first navigate through any websites to determine which are most suitable to meet the objectives for your lessons.

Starfall "Where children have fun learning to read": <www.starfall.com> (accessed March 27, 2009)

Story Place: The children's digital library <www.storyplace.org> (accessed March 27, 2009)

Scholastic Kids: <http://www.scholastic.com/kids/stacks/> (accessed March 27, 2009)

Section Three

Writing Our Way into Literature Using Multimedia and Digital Technology

Chapter 6

Being, Becoming, and Belonging: An Integrated Literacy Approach

Miriam Davidson and Mary Ladky

> The self is a text; it has to be deciphered.... The self is a project, something to be built. (D.H. Lawrence)

Middle and secondary school students' literacy skills have been, and currently are, the subject of much concern, and the debate over how best to support their development continues. As well, the increasing democratization of education demands that teachers develop a diverse toolbox of practices that address the needs of each student, often exceedingly variable in both elementary and intermediate settings. Understanding the nature of adolescent literacy is complex, and within the past ten years, regular shifts have occurred between the need for teachers to emphasize functional skills and provide quantifiable results from tracking mechanisms and, conversely, the value of developing student voice and empowering creativity, especially when attempting to capture the interest of disengaged students.

When children move out of primary classrooms into the upper elementary grades (grades 4, 5, and 6), their learning becomes increasingly fragmented, as each mode of communication or dimension of literacy is presented in increasing isolation. Most books for older children are devoid of illustrations, the element that they cherished in the earlier grades, and the visual arts are taught separately, removed from any context except perhaps the rhythm of yearly seasons or holiday themes. In an effort to improve and support literacy, language arts activities for upper elementary and intermediate students focus on spelling, comprehension, and vocabulary building and leave behind more creative, personally meaningful, or integrated writing activities.

We have outlined in this chapter a response to these issues, a response based on a year-long collaborative approach to supporting and enriching the literacy of a group of intermediate students. We followed a "transmediation" process (Siegel 1995; 2006) to encourage students to move seamlessly between different forms of expression. Rather than addressing each literacy skill in isolation, we worked toward a fluid movement between talk, visual imagery, and the written word. Using photography, a highly accessible art form, and a selection of literary texts as springboards, students broke through their resistance to school-based writing (Elbow 200), finding confidence in their voices and making progress in their overall literacy skills.

Royal Street School (names of school and students are pseudonyms) was constructed at the start of the 20th century. With deep red brick and stone pillars, the original façade could be described as stately, designed to give the impression that something important is taking place inside its walls. Now rather less grand, the world inside those walls has been transformed into a noisy, busy echo chamber where modern voices — those of students and teachers alike — ring out. In this environment, even the most earnest teachers and learners are challenged.

The student population at Royal Street School is made up of two distinct communities — one community is the student population enrolled in the French immersion stream. Students in the French immersion stream, which begins in junior kindergarten, come primarily from stable middle-class homes where parents and guardians have fairly positive relationships with formal learning environments. Teachers, parents, and administrators all tacitly view the immersion students as more academically capable than those in the English stream and, therefore, denotations of privilege pervade their discourse which, in turn, trickles down to the students' regard for themselves.

The children with whom we worked in Room 7 represented a cross-section of the students enrolled in the English stream at Royal Street School. This class had students with quite sophisticated academic skills as well as those who required significant support, both academically and socially. Working with this disparate group was a challenge; however, their curiosity, inquisitiveness, excitement, and even their resistance intrigued us.

The students at Royal Street School did not receive regular instruction in visual arts; therefore, their competence in and comfort level with art-making reflected their individual interests in and experiences with art, which occurred mainly outside school. We decided that photography was the visual medium that would empower the students to conceive of themselves as image-makers. Photography provides accessibility and connection to the world outside the classroom through advertising, sports, popular culture, and the Internet, all of which make it a relevant and engaging medium for contemporary youth. Our goal was to have the children make a personal investment in the image-making process, which required us to adopt a rigorous approach to the teaching of photography. Photography could provide the students with a direct means of observing, selecting, framing, and recording their experiences.

Our project with the students of Room 7 began in the spring of 2007 and continued for a year, as scheduling allowed. Our first goal was to produce a magazine featuring a selection of photographs and written narratives created by the students. To support the purchase of the cameras, film, and journals that we used in the project, we obtained university grants. Using these funds, we provided each student with a new 35mm point-and-shoot camera, to be considered on loan for the duration of the project, and several rolls of 24-exposure colour film that included processing. When we assigned these materials to students, we asked them to sign a Camera and Journal Care—Student Contract (see Figure 6.5, page 69) that outlined their responsibilities for the use and maintenance of the cameras and journals. One of the remarkable aspects of working with this group was their obvious appreciation for the materials provided.

Although familiar with photography, especially cell phone cameras or other digital devices, few of these students had any hands-on experience using a 35mm camera, even a basic one. Therefore, we spent considerable time helping them master basic camera operation, viewing photographs from a range of genres and discussing the aesthetics of those images. Our demonstrations included careful instruction in how to load and unload film, to read and understand all electronic displays, how to work with the flash, and how to hold the camera correctly while shooting.

Along with the camera, each student received a hardcover writing journal, which was theirs to keep and theirs to share only if they wished. These journals had lined pages with clear pockets in the back and front, perfect for storing their 4 x 6 prints. Our first activities focused on making the journals their own; for example, students designed a cover page that included their name as an acrostic poem. Although our original goal was to have students write personal narratives as part of the magazine project, we had to adjust our expectations when we realized that many students resisted writing in any form at all, or if they did write, the work was painfully error-ridden and short.

As a result, we centred the reading activities on appreciation of a selection of structured poetic forms like haiku and inference poems. We approached these forms of writing as we did the photography, by encouraging the students to learn the "language" of writing. We provided a list of poetic terms such as alliteration, consonance, metaphor, and repetition. To prove the value of familiarizing themselves with these terms, we then gave them copies of a few current pop songs and asked them to search for and identify the poetic forms used by the songwriters. Thereafter, we spent some time reading a selection of short poems, among them "Backdrop Addresses Cowboy" by Margaret Atwood, and a selection of haiku from *The Poet's Pen: Writing Poetry with Middle and High School Students* (Lies 1993). These explorations encouraged students to employ a variety of short poetic forms, like haiku, in response to their own photographic images. These images included the self, home and family, and community and the environment. Eventually, the students developed themes that began to guide them in their writing.

In their first images, many of the students paid little attention to composition, viewpoint, lighting, or other aesthetic elements introduced in our first few sessions together. Nevertheless, when commenting on these photographs and the students' initial forays into writing, we did so with a seriousness that seemed alien to them. The weekly sharing sessions, usually involving both one-on-one and small-group work, allowed time to remark on the outstanding visual compositions or written work. This stage was important for all the children, but especially so for those not used to being praised for their work. They so enjoyed viewing their own images enlarged on the screen that their joy stimulated conversation. In some cases, their dialogue sparked the creation of new written texts to accompany their images. The formatting and presentation of their work in a professional manner was key in evoking these responses—they were surprised by the quality of their own work and by the attention that we gave it.

This more fluid, flexible structure that evolved with the students of Room 7 runs counter to much beginner level programming, where open-ended activities are reserved for more experienced or advanced students. The opposite worked best for the students at Royal Street School. By starting with a very self-directed approach, then moving on to more directed activities, students became increasingly invested in the project and confident of their contributions.

The gradual but evident improvement in their image-making helped support the writing activities, particularly for some of the most disengaged students. Working directly from their photographic images led these students to talk more openly and then to write with more confidence and interest. The example below of Nathan's writing originated from the image of an old stone stairway going down into a river. On film, he captured the river, the changing landscape, and an autumn sky reflected in the deep blue water of the river.

Figure 6.1.

Memories Disappearing

Worn like the old stairway.
I see a blurred reflection of myself,
in the water that now covers it.
I imagine how great that stairway once was,
dreaming I was there to experience it.
The stairway is cracked and rough,
But this doesn't make it weak or useless.
Each crack and chip tells a different story.
Memories disappearing.

—by Nathan

Figure 6.2.

For Susan, an extremely reticent writer, it was her deep affection for her younger twin brothers and a wonderful series of portraits she made of them that gave her the confidence to write with emotion and physicality.

My Baby Brother

Kevin is really adorable and small.
He can climb like a monkey.
His eyes make you melt.
When he was born,
I was scared to hold him;
I thought he would break.
He was red as an apple.
His legs propelling him like a cyclist.

—by Susan

When we realized that the students had very little experience having their work presented in a professional manner and shared with the community outside their classroom, we decided that an excellent way to wrap up the first part of our collaboration would be to design and produce a magazine printed on high quality paper. The idea of such a publication provided the students with a tangible goal to work toward—a product that would reflect their ideas and their efforts. To focus them on the different elements of the magazine, we divided the students into three small design teams—visual design, writing, and layout—which allowed all students to have a voice in the process. Each "voice" took time and steady encouragement to develop, but the team effort worked well for those students more reluctant to invest in the project. Their collaboration continued in the fall term with the promise of a public exhibition to take place in the city's public art gallery. The idea of moving their work outside the school and into the larger community empowered the students and helped them recognize and celebrate their worthiness (Fried 2001).

While the two intermediate teachers worked with the students in small groups on literacy activities, our time with the students was spent helping them select photographs for the exhibit and develop new writing with a focus on the theme of transformation. This theme related well to the fall season, the changing leaves, the transition to winter, and the students' own progress into their final year at school. The exhibition was scheduled to open in early November, allowing us just two months to prepare. With this event on the horizon, students began to work with more determination and commitment. The positive experience of seeing their work formatted and published in the first magazine we put together helped them to imagine just how impressive an exhibition of their photographs and writing could be. Their sense of their own literacy began to expand and take root as a result of this "more worldly transaction between text and reader" (Elbow 2000, 33).

A year later...

Almost a year after we first met the children of Room 7, we began our final project with them, which involved the production of a mixed media self-portrait and, afterwards, a piece of writing that creatively explored the chosen focus of the portrait. The public dimension of this phase was the school's end-of-year Arts Café, an evening event celebrating the artistic accomplishments of the students, which was open to the community. It functioned as a kind of good-bye to the students' elementary school experience. As part of the event, photographs and writing from the earlier exhibition at the city art gallery were also shown. At this stage, the students were finally ready to engage in a transmediated process, translating the interplay between their photographic skills, their understanding of two works of children's literature, and their own written work.

To get them started on planning the visual portion of their project, we showed the students examples of different approaches to the creation of a mixed media self-portrait, with a particular emphasis on those that integrated photography in interesting ways. This time, we suggested the broad topics of their hopes and dreams for the future, but encouraged the students to explore other aspects of their identity, including hobbies and family, if they wished. We selected two works of children's literature to trigger their interest in the idea of identity formation and to provide some of the language for writing about the self-portraits they created.

We read *Tar Beach* (Ringgold 1991) and *Talking Walls* (Burns Knight 1995) aloud to the students in small groups and discussed them as texts that explore aspects of identity—being a child, belonging to a family and to a community, and the process of becoming something not clearly known yet or fully understood.

In *Tar Beach*, Faith Ringgold recounts the dream adventure of eight-year-old Cassie Louise Lightfoot, who flies above her apartment-building rooftop, the "tar beach" of the title, looking down on 1939 Harlem. The book is part autobiographical and part fictional, and it uses the metaphor of flight to help recount the challenges presented to her African-American ancestors, and to her hopes and dreams for the future. In *Talking Walls*, the author Margy Burns Knight and illustrator Anne Sibley O'Brien explore the idea that each of us has a story to tell and a heritage worth preserving. By telling the stories of walls around the world—the Great Wall of China, Nelson Mandela's prison walls, the Peace Lines in Belfast, Northern Ireland—they show how walls can hold a community together or separate it. The book succeeds by broadening children's understanding of other cultures in a non-judgmental way. Our students listened to these stories carefully, drawn particularly to the idea that identity is multi-faceted and individual, but not completely written in stone.

The self-portraits took several sessions of more than 90 minutes to design and complete. After planning their compositions, each student received a piece of high quality 12" x 18" illustration board onto which they transferred their designs. The self-portraits were a mix of drawn imagery, collaged materials, and photographs that we shot on-site using a digital camera and portable printer. The process was very exciting for the children as they were able to pose for their photographs, have their pictures taken, then print them out, all on-site. Their photos were then cut out and collaged into the scenes that the children created.

The students used their self-portraits and the visual media available to them to articulate their ideas in a range of visual styles, including abstract collages and painterly images, as well as cartoon-like or highly representational compositions. As their work on the self-portraits progressed, the children regularly requested that we track down specific imagery—images of popular musical performers, cartoon and video game characters, famous athletes, the instruments that they play, and exotic locations around the world, including

Figure 6.3. Emily considering how to incorporate images of herself, posed in a variety of different dance positions, into her self-portrait composition.

places they hoped to visit in the future—all to be included in their compositions. Additionally, they had access to magazine images and a wide array of visual art materials such as watercolour pencils, pastels, permanent markers, adhesives, watercolour paints and brushes, tissue paper and other specialty papers to help them to realize their ideas in a variety of ways.

As in earlier phases of our work together, we encouraged the students to move between literary texts, language, and images in a seamless fashion, understanding the multi-dimensionality of each. Some students were directly inspired by the two books while others wrote more specifically to the subject of their self-portraits. Emily was one student who drew the flying metaphor from *Tar Beach* and wove it into her visual self-portrait, which explored her love of dance:

> *The sky's the limit when your heart's in it*
>
> On stage there's a freedom to move however you want, no boundaries.
> In the air there would be the same freedom to be able to go wherever you want.
> But I'm not ready to fly. My suitcase isn't packed yet.
> For now, I will stick to the stage and the classroom.
> The sky's the limit when your heart's in it.
> Think of the places I could go and the things I could do.
> My plane could land near a vast populated skyline or it could land where the heat from the sun is all the heat you need.
> Anywhere.
>
> —by Emily

Robert, on the other hand, oriented his visual self-portrait toward a future aspiration, using props to fully express his career hopes. His writing is playful and optimistic—a reflection of the hopeful young person we had come to know, a boy who had clearly matured and developed his own voice through this project:

Figure 6.4.

Cooking with Chef Robert

The burner heats up. The fire roars. The food sizzles on the frying pan.
Smells of great food and good times waft from the kitchen where the
  true magic happens.
Because it's not how the food is served or how nice the service is
But it matters how it's made and presented.
That's what really makes the difference.
But before any of that happens, there is a recipe to be made that sets out
The way everything is to be done and how to do it.

—by Robert

Offering students the opportunity to direct and construct forms of self-expression—visually and through written language—increases their sense of themselves as active producers of their literacy education rather than just passive consumers or readers of text. The rewards of such opportunities are numerous. The intermediate students at Royal Street School who took part in this enrichment program were clearly grateful for the obvious benefits that included the development of their photographic skills, the use and care of a camera, two student-generated magazines, a professionally matted colour enlargement of their exhibition photo to keep as well as their self-portrait, and finally, the chance for their work to be celebrated in two public exhibitions. Our emphasis on requiring professional quality work from them met with less resistance when they understood that their work was going to be seen and appreciated well beyond their teachers and their grade books.

A number of these students decided to apply to the integrated arts program at their local secondary school and were accepted into the visual arts stream for the next year. Others simply gained a sense of pride that their voices—their creative output—mattered. In this regard, one student went so far as to email Ryerson University's Imaging Arts Program, sending along samples of his photographs. He received strong affirmation in the form of a letter from Ryerson, stating that his work showed promise and encouraging him to apply to their program when he completed high school. These outcomes are significant.

Similar outcomes can be accomplished by teachers in a variety of ways, but when the relationship between image-making and creative writing processes are explicit, it is highly motivating, especially for those students who struggle with some aspect of their literacy development. Their motivation is further enhanced when the visual medium that students employ is directly connected to their experiences outside the classroom, through books, film, television, MTV, video game narratives, and the Internet. The highly democratic and familiar nature of photography makes it an excellent choice when working to engage students in their writing. However, teachers do not need to have photographic expertise or camera equipment available. Found photographs, family albums, travel images, school pictures, popular media images can be effectively employed to support students' writing practices.

That being said, Royal Street students' investment in the activities was enhanced because they created the visual material we asked them to write about. This, in conjunction with explorations of a variety of literary texts, led the students to develop themes that helped them reflect upon their personal environments, their relationships with friends and family members, their histories, their communities, and their dreams for the future. This sense of control and choice was vital to moving these students toward a deeper connection with, and belief in, their own communicative potential. If teachers are to support all students in the development of literacy skills, they must provide the time and the space for them to "decipher the self" (Lawrence 1925). These multimodal approaches provide rich possibilities and are an essential addition to the challenging project of helping students become literate and engaged members of their community.

Camera and Journal Care—Student Contract
Photography and Creative Writing Project

Instructor _____

CAMERA

On Tuesday, April 10, 2007, I received an Olympus Stylus Epic 35mm camera and case, which is on loan from _____.

This camera can be used for the duration of the project and will be returned to _____ when the project is complete so that it can be used in future work with students at Royal Street School and other local schools.

    Camera # _____

    Serial # _____

I agree to care for and maintain this camera to the very best of my ability. I will make sure that I keep it with me at all times or store it in a safe place in my home or at school with my classroom teacher.

I realize that this camera is on loan to me and I promise to do my very best to ensure that it stays in good working order.

I will retain all the negatives and photographic prints that I create through this project.

JOURNAL

On Tuesday, April 10, 2007, I received a journal that I will use to house the writing and photographs I produce in this project. I will use this journal to work on creative writing projects and to display/store the 4- x 6-inch prints of my photographs.

I will do my very best to ensure that I do not lose my journal.

I will make sure that I keep my journal with me at all times or store it in a safe place in my home or at school.

I realize that it is extremely important that I bring my journal with me to each of our photography and writing workshops that take place on Tuesday and Thursday afternoons.

I will retain my personal journal and all the photographs that are included in it at the end of the project.

I , _____ , have read and agreed to the terms outlined above. I will do my best to ensure the care of both my camera and my journal.

    Signed: _____

    Dated: _____

Figure 6.5.

REFERENCES

Burns Knight, Margy, and Anne Sibley O'Brien, illustr. 1995. *Talking walls*. Gardiner, Maine: Tilbury House.

Elbow, Peter. 2000. *Everyone can write: Essays toward a hopeful theory of writing*. New York: Oxford University Press.

Ewald, Wendy, and Alexandra Lightfoot. 2002. *I wanna take me a picture: Teaching photography and writing to children*. Boston: Beacon Press.

Ewald, Wendy, and M. Tingley. 2002. *The best part of me: Children talk about their bodies in pictures and words*. New York: Little Brown.

Fried, Robert L. 2001. *The passionate teacher: A practical guide*, 2nd ed. Boston: Beacon Press.

Hooks, Bell. 1994. *Teaching to transgress: Education as a practice of freedom*. London: Routledge.

Janeczko, P. B. 2005. *A kick in the head: An everyday guide to poetic forms*. Cambridge: Candlewick Press.

Lawrence, D.H. 1925. *Art and orality*. The Calendar of Modern Letters, vol. 2., No. 10.

Lies, Betty Bonham. 1993. *The poet's pen: Writing poetry with middle and high school students*. Portsmouth, NH: Teachers Ideas Press.

Ringgold, Faith. 1991. *Tar Beach*. New York: Crown Books.

Siegel, Marjorie. 1995. More than words: The generative potential of transmediation for learning. *Canadian Journal of Education*, 20.4, 455–475.

Siegel, Marjorie. 2006. Rereading the signs: Multimodal transformations in the field of literacy education. *Language Arts*, 84.1, 65–77.

RESOURCES

Websites

For a selection of poems including Margaret Atwood's *Backdrop addresses cowboy*, go to Out Loud: National Poetry Recitation Project: <http://poetryoutloud.org/poems/> (accessed March 27, 2009).

For more information on photographic projects in schools and communities, visit the Center for Documentary Studies at Duke University— Projects link <http://cds.aas.duke.edu/docprojects/index.html> (accessed March 27, 2009), and

Venice Arts in Neighborhoods: <http://www.venice-arts.org> (accessed March 27, 2009).

Chapter 7

Art-Full Journals: Making Multimodal Connections

Jane Baskwill

> Mark[1]: Well, it's about accepting people for who they are. I mean, I tried to show that it's not what's on the outside. That's why I have the people open up kind of … like you can't tell what's inside a book by just looking at its cover. You know, like you have to read it to know if you are going to like it. Well I thought I would try to show that by … um … making my people open too—like books.

Mark is sharing an entry from his art-full reflective journal with a group of his grade 4 classmates during an exploration of the text set[2] we called *Finding Our Way* (see page 81), which included approximately twenty picture books that brought together issues of diversity, racism, conflict, and friendship along with illustrations that were compelling and evocative.

An art-full reflective journal is a space where students create visual texts using a variety of mediums such as drawing, collage, photographs, and watercolour along with written responses of varying lengths and types (poetry, narrative, quotations). It is a constantly evolving and changing space in which to represent, confront, explore, and challenge personal beliefs and assumptions—in this case, about multicultural picture books.

Many teachers, particularly in Language Arts, ask their students to keep journals in which they record their responses to the literature they are reading. But I have found that traditional response journals lose their

---

[1] The names of participants have been changed to protect their privacy.

[2] A **text set** is a collection of print materials (books, magazines, flyers) and media texts (video segments, DVDs, YouTube clips, podcasts, blogs, and similar sources). The texts should have some meaningful relationship between and among them and, for the purposes of this project, the picture books that anchor each text set should have the potential to evoke powerful responses from the reader.

potential for impact because students see them as an assignment for the teacher, not as a space in which they can investigate their own thinking and create their own knowledge. Perhaps journals have become too commonplace or, with too many restrictive rules applied, school-like—an assignment to be marked, not a tool for learning. In contrast, I have found that keeping an art-full journal is a transformative experience for both students and teachers, especially if teachers create their own art-full responses along with their students. The journals provide a safe space in which to wrestle with "big ideas" such as diversity, poverty, racism, democracy, freedom, friendship, peace, and power. They become the space in which students can capture visually what they might otherwise struggle to convey in words alone. Using words with visual images is a powerful way to examine personal connections between multicultural picture books and lived experience.

I introduced the art-full journal to Anna's grade 4 class (all names are pseudonyms) by bringing in some journals prepared by graduate teachers in my university children's literature classes.[3] As I showed the journals, there were appreciative comments about the techniques used and questions why the journal owner created the page the way they did. The class was a-buzz with anticipation and excitement when Anna and I informed the students they would be using art-full journals of their own to respond to text sets of books on a variety of themes. The class was already used to making text-to-text, text-to- self, and text-to-world connections to their readings, so I was able to use their experience as a point of reference. We talked about the terms "connections" and "visual representation." Anna and I weren't sure if they were grasping the idea or not until Jamie summed up our explanation and expressed his understanding for our benefit and that of his classmates: "Oh," he said thoughtfully. "You mean you want to see what we're thinking!" This seemed to be one of those "light bulb" moments for the whole class. Anna and I were certain that Jamie had put us on the right track.

In deciding how to organize the time the students would spend with their journals, Anna and I drew on our teaching experience with writers' workshop and the work of several key teacher educators. We looked to the writings of Donald Graves, Lucy Calkins, and Shelley Harwayne. Graves taught us about the importance of dedicating time for writer's workshop. From Calkins, we learned about using writer's notebooks and helping students generate ideas during conferences. Harwayne helped us with mini-lessons and demonstrations. I also connected to the work of Karen Ernst who used a writers' workshop approach in the art classroom. Anna and her students became immersed in an environment of thoughtful reflection and connection where each member of the class was supportive of each other's efforts. Uninterrupted time in order to plan, create, and connect with each other's work was a necessary ingredient.

---

[3] There are a number of excellent websites with examples of visual journals that can be used in lieu of in-hand examples. There are also some useful how-to books. See References at end of this chapter.

Anna and I looked at her timetable for a place in the curriculum in which to locate this work. There are many topics in social studies and science that afford a natural link and for which appropriate and engaging text sets can be assembled—such topics as the "discovery" of North America, the struggles and contributions of First Nations, the Holocaust, wars past and present, environmental issues, and endangered species, to name a few. Anna was comfortable with an interdisciplinary approach so we wove together time from language arts, social studies, and, most naturally, art in order to give students enough time for connecting, composing, and sharing. Anna felt she could devote 45 minutes a day, three times a week, to art-full journaling, though we quickly found that we were looking for additional time.

I also put together collections of multicultural text sets around a number of "big ideas." For the purpose of this chapter, I focused on the picture books that formed the art-full cornerstone of our text sets. However, as we worked with these picture books, other texts made their way into our collection (newspapers, magazines, videos, DVDs, audio files, websites, personal notes, emails, photos, and other artifacts). As the students began to make connections, they found everyday texts and brought in URLs for websites, blogs, audio and video files, and even some of their own emails and text messages that they felt should be considered. We were conscious of the need to question some Internet content so we always previewed them in advance to make sure the content was appropriate. Text sets shift the "knowing" from the text to the learner, and they provide the springboard for multimodal ways of knowing and representing knowledge.

The picture books we used were what I considered to be strong texts. Although there are no hard and fast rules for their selection, because selection depends on the teacher's objectives, we used the following criteria:

1. **Enthusiasm**: This was a gut-level response to our first reading. If we liked it, we felt it would ignite students' interest and curiosity.
2. **Suitability**: The book needed to be appropriate to some aspect of the broader topic/theme.
3. **Connectivity**: There were possibilities for broad connections to other texts and to students' personal or family experiences, and/or global issues.
4. **Quality**: We wanted books that were well written with rich language and artful illustrations.
5. **Diversity**: We looked for books that represented diverse populations and points of view, or that dealt with an issue from multiple perspectives.
6. **Deeper meaning**: We searched for books that could be read for multiple meanings and that could lead students to deeper meanings around ways of being in the world.

We collected multiple copies of many of the selected books so we would have ample resources available whenever the students might want to refer to

Topics and Intended Outcomes for Visual Literacy
Mini-lessons using Picture Book Illustrations

Topic	Intended Outcomes
Media (paint, pencil, collage, and so on)	• Compare media using picture book illustrations. • Describe how choice affects the look.
Design (shape, line, texture, contrast, pattern, colour, space)	• Identify types of shapes used—geometric, organic, repetitive. • Identify types of lines—thin, thick, squiggly, straight, short. • Identify examples of textures—rough, smooth, feathery—and examine how the artist created it. • Identify examples of strong light and dark contrast. • Identify examples of colour—subdued, bright, tinted, shaded, transparent, solid. • Identify how space is shown—deep (showing depth) or flat.
Subject	• Identify how the theme is portrayed. • Compare illustrations by different illustrators of the same story. • Identify variations.
Impact	• Describe your reaction in terms of media, design, subject.

Figure 7.1.

them. We decided to introduce the books by reading each of them aloud. We also made audio recordings of the books for use at a listening centre.[4]

Not unlike writer's workshop, we conducted mini-lessons (see pages 84–86) on art-full techniques and how to respond to each other's work. Figure 7.1 (above) provides a list of possible topics and intended outcomes for such mini-lessons. We asked the students to pay attention to the details (Figure 7.2), to see the "small" inside the "big." We also showed them how to capture their connections (Figure 7.3) in sketches, words, phrases, or short paragraphs—either on their own or from the book—as they read. We asked them to pay attention also to the sensory connections they were making. These "notes" provided students with a beginning point from which to make their art-full connections and reflections during our workshop time.

We also compiled a list of sample questions for the students to use when sharing their journals (Figure 7.4). We generated this list with the students and added to it over the course of our work together. We posted it on chart paper and also made it into a bookmark that was given to each student to keep for ready reference.

Anna and I also put together what we called an artist's toolkit, our own version of a "tickle trunk" into which we put a variety of art supplies—chalk, coloured pencils, paint, a selection of textured papers like corrugated

---

[4] Recordings can be made using whatever technology your school has available (tape or digital recorder, or computer). Use the Record function on your computer for creating audio files. The computer will become a listening station. Add headphones for individual students or an actual listening centre for multiple users. Whatever device you use, keep it simple in order to allow the maximum number of books to be recorded in the shortest space of time.

cardboard, tissue paper, and wallpaper. Many of these supplies were scrounged from print shops, yard sales, and our own homes, and we sent a letter home so parents could be on the lookout for the list of supplies.

We integrated new technologies whenever appropriate. Just as we did with art and response techniques, we conducted mini-lessons and demonstrations to show students how they might use various technologies. We showed students how to use digital photography to capture their ideas and emotions by looking at the work of photographers and discussing what connections their images evoked. They learned how to create photo essays (a series of photos that tell a story) and how to use images to represent bigger ideas. For example, students one at a time took the digital camera home with the challenge to take photos to represent an abstract idea such as hope, love, friendship. When they returned, we showed their photos to the class, using the computer and LCD projector, and had the photographer share why they chose their particular subject matter. They learned to crop photos, position them, and even altered their colour. We showed all students how to use the features in Microsoft Word and Photoshop and incorporate these techniques, although we allowed them to determine when it was appropriate to use them.

> **SAMPLE QUESTIONS FOR PEER-SHARING OF ART-FULL JOURNAL RESPONSES**
>
> - How did you create this piece?
> - Did you have any problems? What were they?
> - Why did you choose this style?
> - What is your piece about?
> - What connections did you make?
> - Is there anything you would do differently?
> - Can you tell me more about _____? (style, colours, your connections)
> - How do you hope people will feel when they view this piece?
> - What did you connect with in this piece?
> - What did this piece make you wonder about?
> - What did you really like about this work?
> - What suggestions do you have?
>
> **Figure 7.4.**

Making personal connections: Linking family stories

We used a text set of books from different times and cultures (see pages 81 to 83). The main characters were hopeful, proud, and compassionate, and they were able to forge relationships despite their age differences. We encouraged the children to bring artefacts from home that they felt connected with the books or characters in this set. Anna and I met with the students, individually and in small groups, in order to understand their thinking and the connections they were making. Many of the students connected with the books on a personal level. The books became the topic of conversation in their homes and led them to do their own investigations of what growing up was like for their parents, their grandparents, and their great grandparents.

George connected what he was reading to his grandmother's experiences:

> "I ... asked my Gran what her story was. I didn't know that she lived on a farm ... see (shows photo). She had to do lots of chores—before and after school! Hard chores, too. She said her dad was disappointed when she was born. He thought a boy would be more helpful on the farm. He said they were stronger.... She said she proved she could work just as hard as the boys."

Similarly, Julie's artefact connected her to her great-grandmother in a more tangible way:

> "I was talking to my grandmother and she had a letter that belonged to her mother—my great-grandmother. Look at the fancy writing. I can hardly read it but she is writing about a trip she and her family took to the Boston states. I'm not sure why they called it that. Mom says it's just Boston—you know—the city. It was a big deal in those days to go that far away."

Just as pre-writing activities help prime the pump for writing, small-group discussions about the books, the characters, and the artefacts do the same for art-full journal responses. Issues such as gender equity, fairness, sexism, and ageism entered the conversation and took on new meaning as they were now connected to actual family events. Everyday events like travel, communication, and even the birth of a baby generated more interest and were more meaningful when juxtaposed against family stories and experiences. A few days later, the children's journals reflected both their discussions and reading and demonstrated how they were moving from connecting personally to connecting on a wider, more global scale.

George's style was reminiscent of *A Birthday Basket for Tia*. He had cut papers from a variety of textures and glued them on his page as the background. On to this paper field, he glued a large torn paper tree with the faces of several older people cut out of magazines and glued on the trunk. One large branch had broken off the tree and rested against the trunk. Around the tree were paper doll children in groups of two or three. One child, cut from a magazine, was standing close to the tree. A white square of paper was glued near the hands of this child. On the paper were words that I recognized as coming from *Mrs. Katz and Tush*—"Such a person." George had this to say about his piece:

> "I got to thinking about how old people are kind of like old trees—they've seen a lot in their lives. That's why I put the tree here and the faces—to show I'm makin' a connection like. And then I thought me and my friends didn't take much notice before. See? (He points to the groups of children playing.) But now I'm kinda noticin' more so here I am close to the tree and all. And I remembered Mrs. Katz kept sayin' those words over and over and how they put them on her stone and all so I thought I should use them too—for *all* the old people—you know, they're, they're, such persons!"

George used the metaphor of the tree to represent what he had learned about the value of older people. He showed that his reading had an impact on his attitude and thinking, and that he had made this change himself, without necessarily having the support of his friends. He also was cognizant of this growing awareness. George connected and re-connected with one book in particular and demonstrated his awareness of how that book (*Mrs. Katz and Tush*) had influenced his art-full response.

Julie shared how a tradition (a story cloth) from one culture can have meaning and value for another. Julie's page was covered with a sheet of coloured paper onto which she had painstakingly drawn what looked like stitches. On closer inspection, there was a story being told on the page:

> "I really wanted to stitch a cloth, a pa'ndau like in *The Whispering Cloth* but I thought it would take me too long so I drew my stitches on instead. Maybe I will actually stitch it—for my grandmother for Christmas. My mom says she can show me how. She does embroidery. She says it's a lot like that. Anyway, I show the story of my great-grandmother and her trip to the Boston states. I show her first over here when she was little and growing up in the country and then going to school for the first time. And over here she is playing with her friends. And over here she goes by boat to Boston with her mom and dad. I really like the idea of having a whispering cloth with stories of a person's life. My great-grandmother didn't have a life like Mai and her grandmother had—they weren't refugees or anything—but they did stuff. I think what I learned is everybody has a story, you know, like their life *is* a story and all and making a cloth lets you show that story."

Julie recognized that personal stories link her with others. Julie also demonstrated how stories can be visual as well as oral, and how one complements the other; one can make a visual record of events and that will become an historical artefact that itself tells a story.

Walking in another's shoes: The development of empathy

With our final text set, The Colour of Home, we asked students to connect with the immigrant experience and the difficulties of moving to a new place and learning a new language. There were school experiences and family situations, representing a variety of cultures.

These students developed empathy from their aesthetic experiences, which gave them a heightened ability to perceive and understand others' points of view. They developed a closeness to the characters and their experiences, connected them across texts and to their own and others' personal experiences.

Callie created a watercolour backdrop onto which she glued drawings of buildings. Her explanation illustrates her thinking:

> "I never thought about how different it is to grow up in other places and stuff. I guess I thought that most kids just grow up ... you know, have toys, x-box, computers, go to the mall, and birthday parties. But now I think about stuff differently, you know, like kids come from all kinds of lives and like the "colours of home" can be ... like ... different and yet there are so many things that are ... like ... the same."

Callie demonstrated her growing awareness of the commonalities and differences among cultures and even within her own community or peer group. She was beginning to make connections with others around these linkages.

Caleb used a pencil to draw what looked like a number of scenes. Some appeared to be school events, while others were home or community. Caleb connected with the books at a very personal level. He came to Canada when he was five years old and, after having heard only Japanese spoken, he was plunged into an English-only environment. As a result, he had a struggle to learn to read and write, which left him with strong memories.

> "I know just how it feels (to learn English). See this ... I drew myself at school and the other kids laughing at me because I couldn't read. I tried, but I just couldn't get it ... it was so hard and I couldn't read like the others. I hated school. And it wasn't just school ... even on the playground kids made fun. Then there was home too, I mean they didn't make fun of me but they wondered why I didn't try harder. Things are better now ... but I know how it feels ... it feels bad."

Caleb was able to empathize with the characters in the picture books and connect with the emotional circumstances of their situations. He was also able to share a very important and highly personal experience publicly with his family and classmates. His visual images enabled him to find his voice. He spoke with confidence—something Anna said he had not done previously. When Caleb was provided with an outlet for the feelings he had previously kept hidden, these feelings were appreciated, respected, and validated by his classmates—as is illustrated by Cassie's reaction. Caleb's poignant and honest response prompted Cassie to refer back to her journal response to the Intergenerational text set.

In response to this theme, Cassie had used coloured pencils and watercolours to draw a picture of an older woman in a long dress which she glued onto a black circle in the centre of the page. She had written the Korean words from *Halmoni and the Picnic* in speech balloons around the woman. She had cut children from magazines, glued them around the four sides of her page, and wrote speech balloons with questions like "What is she saying?" "Tell her to speak English." "Where is she from?" beside each child:

> "I know I showed this before but I ... I wanted to ... you know, to like ... make a connection with Caleb. When I first made this I wanted to ... show the feelings ... you know ... how it made me feel to read the books.... It
> - made me feel ... lonely ... when you're too shy to speak a new language and all, you don't have anyone to talk to. I said I kind of feel this way in French class, remember? Like ... I'm scared I'll be called on and have to speak

French? I don't want anyone to think I'm dumb or have kids laugh and stuff. So, here I put her (Halmoni) in the middle, on the black paper ... to show she's alone. Here are her words. I put the kids around the edge because they're like a fence keeping her from running away. It made me think she must have felt scared and lonely and that's what I tried to show. But now I think ... I can really connect, you know, outside the book to what Caleb was feeling and it's awesome!"

The strong texts we used over the course of several months evoked multiple meanings for these students, broadened their outlook and appreciation, and opened up imagined possibilities. They engaged in more complex abstract thinking and used higher order thinking skills to develop a deeper understanding and appreciation of the big ideas we had tackled with them. They empathized to take on new perspectives, evaluated character actions, made personal connections, analyzed conflict, and applied critical problem solving in order to represent their connections visually.

Going public

At the end of our twelve weeks, Anna and I discussed with the students how they might share their journals in a more public way. We talked about some options—taking photos of the journal responses and creating a slide show using PowerPoint, or putting the actual journals in the school library for people to view. The students decided to share their journals in the form of an art installation in the school library and to make a slide show for the school's website. Anna and I helped them select particular responses they wanted to feature as examples of their most thoughtful work. We left the interpretation of this up to each student, but asked that they write a short piece that explained, just as they had done during their discussions, a bit about the materials and techniques they used and what connections they had made to the texts. Their final copies were typed using a word-processing program, printed off, and mounted on coloured paper.

We brainstormed information we thought viewers might want or need to know; then we divided the class into small groups to write some information about art-full journaling and the text sets that inspired their work. One group was in charge of posters and advertising and used their word processing skills to create them. The posters were given to another group for illustration and decoration. Still another group was in charge of signage to guide viewers through the installation, and another looked after making arrangements for class visits and set up a schedule in consultation with the teachers and library technician.

Anna and I brought in tablecloths for the tops of the bookshelves and tables. We were given permission for the class to go to the library the afternoon of the day before the showing in order to set up so that everything would be ready for the next day. In addition, a small group of students photographed the selected art-full journal responses and arranged them into a PowerPoint presentation. They presented the slide show to their classmates and sought feedback and suggestions. They emailed the principal to inform her about their project and to find out how to go about getting it on the school's website. Their final product became a "virtual" installation on the site.

Concluding thoughts

When "strong texts" are shared across contexts and across cultures, using "aesthetic interpretive practices" (Barrett 1999), issues of similarities and connection as well as differences come to the fore. When teachers use art-full journals in the classroom they provide their students with powerful tools with which they can express meaning about themselves and others. This understanding is becoming increasingly important in an era of "new educational accountability" and imposed "standards," where curriculum has been sanitized and boiled down to its lowest common denominator.

Figure 7.5.

Art-full journals are gateways through which students can merge "old technologies" (storytelling, literature, drawing, and collage) with the new (digital photography and various computer programs and technologies) to share their work with other audiences, enhance their responses with a spoken text or piece of music, or express their feelings and ideas in other forms (a video, a dance, or a graphic novel). They open up a space in which students can embrace children's literature and its connectivity to the everyday, to their lives, to the lives of others, and to the new media and technologies that are increasingly part of their world. When art-full journals are used in conjunction with new technologies, students expand their meaning-making repertoire, and they can share their work and their thinking with other audiences. When teachers expand their definition of literacy to include multiple possibilities for response, they enable their students to move beyond the status quo, to view their world from multiple perspectives, and to consider alternative realities. When we can imagine things being different, we can begin to act accordingly.

REFERENCES

Barrett, Michèle. 1999. *Imagination in theory: Essays on writing and culture.* New York: New York University Press.

Greene, Maxine. 1973. *Teacher as stranger: Educational philosophy for the modern age.* California: Wadsworth Publishing.

Greene, Maxine. 1995. *Releasing the imagination: Essays on education, the arts, and social change*. San Francisco: Jossey-Bass Education.

Short, Kathy, Gloria Kauffman, and Leslie Kahn. 2000. "I just *need* to draw": Responding to literature across multiple sign systems." *The Reading Teacher*, 54, 160–171.

Winterson, Jeanette. 1996. *Art objects: Essays on ecstasy and effrontery*. Toronto: Random House/Vintage Canada.

RESOURCES

THEME: FINDING OUR WAY

Text sets and selected websites

Baskwill, Jane. 2003. *If peace is…* New York: Mondo Publishing

Dawes, Kwame. 2005. *I saw your face*. New York: Dial Books

Castle, Caroline. 2002. *For every child: The UN Convention for the Rights of the Child*. New York: P. Fogelman Books.

Feelings, Tom (illustr.). 1993. *Soul looks back in wonder*. New York: Puffin

Hamanaka, Sheila (illustr.). 1999. *All the colors of the earth*. New York: Mulberry Books

Katz, Karen. 1999. *The colors of us*. New York: Henry Holt

Khan, Rukhsana. 1999. *Muslim child*. Morton Grove, IL: Albert Whitman & Co.

Levine, Ellen. 1989. *I Hate English!* New York: Scholastic.

Llao, Jimmy. 2006. *The sound of colors: A journey of the imagination*. New York: Little Brown & Co.

Mandelbaum, Pili. 1990. *You be me, I'll be you*. Brooklyn: Kane/Miller Publishers

Morris, Ann. 1990. *When will the fighting stop? A child's view of Jerusalem*. New York: Atheneum

Polacco, Patricia. 1994. *Pink and Say*. New York: Scholastic

Say, Allen. 1991. *Tree of cranes*. Boston: Houghton Mifflin

Shange, Ntozake. 1997. *Whitewash*. New York: Walker & Company (Out of print)

Shea, Pegi D. 1996. *The Whispering cloth: A refugee's story*. New York: St. Martin's Press

Surat, Michele M. 1983. *Angel child, dragon child*. New York: Scholastic

Weaver, Janice. 2006. *The Quilt of belonging: Stitching together the stories of a nation*. Vancouver: Raincoast Books/Maple Tree Press

Selected websites (accessed March 27, 2009).

Profile on Tom Feelings (artist/illustrator): <http://ncanewyork.com/feelings.htm>.

Patricia Polacco (author/illustrator): <http://www.patriciapolacco.com/>.

United Nations Cyber School Bus: <http://www0.un.org/cyberschoolbus/racism2001/orglinks.asp>.

Newspapers around the world: <http://www.thepaperboy.com/>.

BBC Children's Newsround: <http://news.bbc.co.uk/cbbcnews/hi/world/default.stm>

BBC Worldservice: <http://www.bbc.co.uk/worldservice/people/features/childrensrights/index.shtml>.

World Peace Project for Children: <http://www.sadako.org/>.

Google Earth: <http://earth.google.com/>.

THEME: INTERGENERATIONAL
Text Set
Baylor, Byrd. 1997. *The other way to listen.* New York: Simon & Schuster.
Bergoli, Jane. 2004. *The goat lady.* Gardiner, MA: Tilbury House.
Choi, Sook Nyul. 1993. *Halmoni and the picnic.* Boston: Houghton Mifflin.
Hoffman, Mary. 1991. *Amazing Grace.* London: Frances Lincoln Children's Books.
Mathis, Sharon Bell. 1975. *The hundred penny box.* New York: Puffin
Mora, Pat. 1997. *A birthday basket for Tia.* New York: Simon & Schuster
Polacco, Patricia. 1994. *Tikvah means hope.* New York: Dell.
Polacco, Patricia. 1992. *Mrs. Katz and Tush.* New York: Dell.
Say, Allen. 1982. *The bicycle man.* Boston: Houghton Mifflin.
Shea, Pegi. 1996. *The whispering cloth: A refugee story.* Honesdale, PA: Boyds Mills
Trottier, Maxine. 1996. *The tiny kite of Eddie Wing.* New York: Kane/Miller
Yolen, Jane. 1997. *Miz Berlin walks.* New York: Puffin.

Websites (accessed March 27, 2009)
Kids Help Seniors: <http://pbskids.org/zoom/activities/action/way06.html >.

News article Children helping Blitz survivors http://www.yourlocalguardian.co.uk/news/features/display.var.1721533.0.children_help_bring_memories_of_the_blitz_back_to_life.php

Children's Literature Network: Author Profile—Byrd Baylor <http://www.childrensliteraturenetwork.org/birthbios/brthpage/03mar/3-28baylor.html >

Allen Say (author/illustrator) audio interview: <http://www.npr.org/templates/story/story.php?storyId=1147806>

Allen Say, at Embracing the Child: <http://www.embracingthechild.org/Bookspecialsay.htm>.

Hmong textile art: <http://www.quiltersmuse.com/hmong_textile_art.htm>.

Pa'ndau story cloth: <http://content.cdlib.org/ark:/13030/hb867nb57m/>.

Hmong quilts news article: <http://www.hmongnet.org/culture/pandau2.html>.

Pat Mora (author): <http://www.patmora.com/>.

THEME: THE COLOUR OF HOME

Text set

Aliki. 1998. *Marianthe's story: Painted words/spoken memories*. New York: Greenwillow.

Baylor, B. 1994. *The table where rich people sit*. New York: Simon Schuster.

Choi, Y. 2001. *The name jar*. New York: Knopf

Dragonwagon, C. 1990. *Home place*. New York: Scholastic.

English, K. 2000. *Speak English for us Marisol!* New York: Albert Whitman & Co.

Heide, F.P. & Gilliland, J.H. 1990. *The day of Ahmed's secret*. New York: Scholastic.

Hoffman, M. (2003). *The color of home*. New York: Phyllis Fogelman/Penguin Putnam.

Khan, R. (1998). *The roses in my carpets*. New York: Holiday House

Mora, P. (1997) *Thomas and the library lady*. New York: Random House.

Pak, S. (1999). *Dear Juno*. New York: Viking.

Recorvits, H. (2003). *My name is Yoon*. New York: Giroux

Yashima, T. (1993). *The village tree*. New York: The Viking Press.

Wyeth, S. (1998). *Something beautiful*. New York: Dragonfly

Websites (accessed March 27, 2009)

Kids Around the World: <http://www.katw.org/>.

UN information on why schooling is important: <http://cyberschoolbus.un.org/literacy2003/slide1_a.asp>.

Cool Planet: <http://www.oxfam.org.uk/coolplanet/kidsweb/wakeup/index.htm>.

Education in Japan: <http://www.amphi.com/~psteffen/fmf/education.htm>.

Education in Africa: <http://pbskids.org/africa/myworld/index.html>.

Global Movement for Children: <http://www.gmfc.org/>.

Voices of Youth: <http://www.unicef.org/voy/index.php>.

Visual Journals: Online examples and information

<http://jeffcoweb.jeffco.k12.co.us/isu/art/sketchbook.html>.

<http://www.artistsjournals.com/>.

<http://aisling.libsyn.com/index.php?post_id=333995#>. (podcast)

<http://www.kporterfield.com/journal/Illuminations.html>.

<http://thevault.blogspot.com/>.

<http://artinyourheart.blogspot.com/2008/01/fourth-grade-visual-journals.html>(connecting families to the art classroom).

<http://www.northampton.edu/prof_com/artlearn/features/journal_feature.htm>.

Mini-Lesson
Peer Response: Paying Attention to Details

Objective: To help students attend to the details in a visual text when responding to each other's work.

Materials: Samples of student journal responses. Taking photos or scanning the images and then projecting is the best way to allow students to see each journal entry clearly. Alternatively, use samples from the Internet [see resources].

Chart paper with the questions listed below printed on it.

What to do: Ask students what they notice in the piece. Prompt them to talk about the colours used, the mood the piece evokes, the creator's style. Some questions to ask are:

- Does this style remind you of any of the books in our text set? Which ones?

  As students make suggestions and explain the visual connections they are making, encourage them to find the picture books they were reminded of.

- What big idea(s) do you think this piece is about? What makes you think that?
- What do you see in this journal response that you don't think anyone else will see?
- Why do you suppose the writer chose the words he or she did? How do the words help your understanding of this piece?
- What connections did you make to this piece?

  After the students have had a chance to respond, ask the creator to talk about their work by answering the following:

- What do you want us to notice about your work?
- What connections did you hope we would make?
- How did you try to tell us what connections you made?

Time for practice

After involving the whole class in this process for a few pieces, have the students respond to a new piece in their journal. Remind them to refer to the questions on the chart paper. Allow approximately 10–15 minutes for their individual work. Then, have them break into small groups of three or four and share their responses and connections. Encourage them to refer to their journals during the discussion.

Note: Students need not answer every question before sharing. This is a guided practice that can be revisited over a few sessions or as often as needed.

Figure 7.2.

Tips

- Prompt students to express why they are thinking in a particular way, how they came to this thought, what they were trying to get across, who influenced their style. Keep asking students in order to help expand their response vocabulary.

- You may want to do a *Think Aloud* to demonstrate how to respond to student work. This is particularly useful for helping to set the ground rules for peer response.

- Spread the lesson over several sessions to avoid losing student interest. Students need some time to process what they have learned. They will then come to each subsequent session with new understandings and skills, which make for deeper and richer responses over time.

Figure 7.2. (cont'd)

Mini-Lesson

Think Aloud: Making Connections

Objective: To demonstrate to students how to take notes as they make connections while reading—by using sketches, words, and phrases for use in planning their art-full responses to texts.

Materials: Blank poster paper or unlined chart paper
Markers
Overheads (optional)

It is helpful if the students can see the book as you read. You can make overheads of the first few pages of the picture book or you can make a PowerPoint of the pages. Some books are also produced in Big Book format which allows students to see the pages more easily.

How to get started: Remind students what a Think Aloud lesson is by explaining *what* the strategies are that you will be using and *why* each of these strategies is helpful. Also ask them to keep track of *when* you use them as you read the text.

What to do: Read the text to your students and, as you read, model your chosen strategies by stopping—sometimes even in the middle of sentences—to articulate aloud the connection you are making. Show the ways available to you to record that connection by sketching, writing, or recording (for words or short passages captured directly from the book).

Show your connection visually on the chart paper. Be sure to use both sketches and words. Don't worry if you think you can't draw well. You don't have to! The idea is to try to capture your thinking in symbols and text, just as you want your students to do—something that can later be used when planning a journal response piece.

Do as many pages of the book as time and interest allow. Conclude the session by explaining how you might use your notes to create a response page in your art-full journal.

Time for practice: Allow time for students to try using the strategies you have demonstrated to show their connections to one of the books in the text set you are working with. After students have completed visual notes for several pages, divide the class into small groups, and have them share their work with one another.

Tips

- Choose a book with which you are very familiar.
- Prepare ahead. Rehearse some of the connections you plan to share and decide if you will sketch, write, or record.
- Make notes. You might want to jot a few notes on an index card to help you recall them during the lesson.
- Be sure to lay ground rules for the sharing sessions so that students will be respectful of each other's work. Search out rules similar to those used in writers' workshops or other similar group-sharing sessions.

Figure 7.3.

Chapter 8

Cyberwriters: Bringing Historical Fiction into the World of New Literacies
Jeanette Thompson

Cyberwriters was a writing project for young writers (between 11 and 15 years) who wanted to learn to create historical fiction stories using digital images, sounds, and words. Unsworth (2006) has elucidated the need for teachers of literature to connect with the multiliterate worlds of young readers in order to broaden their experience. The aims of the Cyberwriters project were to learn about the multiliterate practices of young people, and to discover ways in which historical fiction could be created using new technologies.

The multiliteracies approach to literacy intends to address social inequities and acknowledge diversity in the community (Unsworth et al. 2005). By locating the workshops in the Museum of the Riverina, a shared community space, children from all types of educational backgrounds were able to participate. The Museum features themed displays, oral histories on video, sensory boxes of objects, installations, historic buildings, wagons, carts to climb over, and costumes to dress up in. When children expressed an interest in a particular object or installation, for instance the Cook's Galley, the museum curator was quick to organize a visit from a community elder who worked on the galley and could tell the children stories of his experiences.

In Australia, as in Canada, the emphasis in many museums and libraries has moved from the storage and classification of bequests to the preservation of the social narratives attached to these significant objects (Collections Council 2001). This is in harmony with a multiliteracies approach to education and a gift for the creation of digital texts. In addition to pictorial images, there are oral histories recorded in diverse dialects and the vernacular of each generation. National museums and libraries are interested in finding new ways of making these heritage collections accessible to young people. The Le@rning Federation, supported by state and federal funding in Australia and New Zealand, provides access to the digital collections of national museums and libraries for educational purposes (Burrows et al. 2007).

There is a wealth of digital material available in sound and visual images, software is freely available from the Internet, and young authors no longer need to be computer programmers to create digital stories. The Cyberwriters project demonstrates ways that children and teachers can work together using simple, free software to edit, capture, and construct stories that reflect their local communities and life-worlds.

The Cyberwriters

The Cyberwriters project began with the visit of international children's author, Catherine Jinks, which was sponsored by the local Writers' Centre. Through a series of school visits and newspaper articles, children were invited to email historical fiction stories to the author. On the basis of these stories, twelve young authors were selected to participate in the Cyberwriters workshops. Catherine provided written feedback on the stories and launched the project in a multimedia presentation at the Museum of the Riverina. She played audio recordings of the music she listened to as she created characters and moods while she wrote her novels. (If authors whom you want to invite are unable to visit your community, they may be available through their websites for online discussions about writing.)

Figure 8.1. Cyberwriters at the Museum of the Riverina in New South Wales, Australia

The map

A "learning by design" pedagogical framework was employed for the 8 two-hour workshops. It consists of immersion, overt instruction, critical analysis, and transformed practice in an order and sequence dictated only by the needs of the learner and evolution of the work in progress (Kalantzis et al. 2002). This emphasis on process rather than product may increase student engagement.

The report, *Motivation and engagement of boys* (Munns et al. 2006), suggests that "curriculum that connects to boys' out-of-school experiential learning and the knowledge networks they find personally meaningful will result in increased emotional engagement in learning, along with positive academic and social outcomes" (45). The boys participating in Cyberwriters were more interested in collaboratively creating texts during school and museum information and communications technology (ICT) sessions, using the software and enjoying the process, than in the distant prospect of publication on the museum website. The museum website is not a place they would normally visit.

Jack confided that he and Brendan entered the project "to get out of work." The classroom teacher allowed them time to work on their photo story during school and was delighted at their participation in the project. Mackey (2002) reports a similar attitude among some adolescents in her case studies. Perhaps this playful tinkering was seen by the boys as just as important as the completion of a finished product? For these boys, tinkering seemed to result in increased self-esteem, some positive recognition at school, and practice in transferable ICT skills. They attended eight weeks of Saturday workshops and were doing far more "work" than they realized, perhaps because it was enjoyable and meaningful.

The journey

For the first workshop, the Cyberwriters met each other and read their original stories around the circle. Each participant was recognized as a worthy participant by virtue of their story having been selected by the independent author. They were not selected on the basis of testing or classroom preconceptions about their abilities. Some of the stories didn't have correct spelling or grammar, but the essence of the narrative had sufficient strength for Catherine to consider these shortcomings as fixable. She explained that professional authors often select stories on the basis of their narrative potential rather than their adherence to genre or prescriptions of text types. Here is an excerpt of Cara's melodramatic tale of a local forensic investigation.

> Mystery Murder
> *The Human Glove*
> by Cara
>
> In 1933 a mystery murder was a foot. A murder so foul that families were slamming their doors, locking up the children and hiding themselves inside their homes. People without families were barricading their windows and doors. All because of the discovery of the Human Glove.

The written feedback from Catherine Jinks was discussed. Thereafter, the workshop facilitator provided feedback on the story drafts by email. This process required explicit instruction on the use of Microsoft Word's editing function, Track Changes. Each version of the document was saved and emailed back and forth as an attachment. Using this simple software, the writer is able to see what has been deleted or added to the draft, and the teacher can tag each alteration with a comment. The writer can then accept or reject any or all of the changes and add their own comments. Scrolling over the comment reveals the date and time the comment was made and by whom. This is very useful for assessment of the progress of the child's work. It also provides a digital record of the online conferences you have had with the child.

Editing and writing conferences via the Internet, or intranet within schools, have many advantages. These allow the teacher and student to time-shift the feedback sessions, and it creates a record, accessible at any time and location, of the drafts and conversations. We found that the use of the Internet for homework is limited by family access agreements and, in some cases, the children had access to the Internet only through their parents' work sites. This meant that emails were sometimes deleted or ignored for long periods of time.

Figure 8.2. Cyberwriters online

Microsoft Photo Story 3 was selected as the software for this project because it is available from the Internet as a free download along with the latest version of Media Player. Microsoft Photo Story 3 is as easy to use as a digital photo album, but it also allows the students to record two separate audio tracks for background sound effects and narration. The text function allows users to type words onto the images. Students can also select the way an image is displayed and the camera movement. The steps in learning Photo Story are easier to follow than those in more expensive and sophisticated video-editing programs (see pages 195–203). The program is also easier for children to learn to manipulate their still images for certain visual effects than to capture and edit movement. Most children were already adept at downloading images from their own digital cameras.

Initially, the children were provided with sample photo stories prepared by pre-service teachers from Charles Sturt University. These photo stories had been designed to teach musical concepts to primary school children. It is important to provide models that are different from the photo story that the students are attempting to create. Models that too closely resemble the topic encourage copy-cat reproductions, and models that are too perfect discourage less-polished attempts. These models were engaging and generated lots of ideas for the use of sound. The first task was for each student to create a photo story about themselves, using their own images and music.

Music plays an important role in the expression of adolescent identity. Audio texts are freely available and an important component of adolescent lifestyle. All of the writers had digital MP3 players and were skilled in sourcing and downloading music. They were familiar with the evocative power of music and integrated it into their creations rather than seeing it as an optional extra. Whereas Catherine Jinks used music to set the mood for her writing, the cyberwriters integrated it into their creative multimodal texts.

Multimodal text advocates such as Healy (2008) argue for the supremacy of digital technologies over print. The next generation of children do not seem to regard the choice as binary—they select both. They assess the value of an object by what it can do for them and how they can use it rather than by some innate historical or cultural quality. Debates about the death of the book are irrelevant when we realize the question facing the classroom teacher is not "either-or" but how to provide "more and then some."

Figure 8.3. Cyberwriter Ambrose discusses with Catherine Jinks the use of music for inspiration.

Mackey (2002) identifies "salience" and "fluency of access" as the two elements that adolescents counterbalance in order to make text choices. This was particularly evident in the case of Angela. She enjoyed the writing sessions and being able to experiment with the technology at the museum. However, she did not persist to complete her photo story at home because download speeds were too slow and she preferred to complete the story as a word document without pictures. Some others found the download, although free, not practical at home. They had very definite preferences for their texts and practices at home.

Not all multimodal literature is digital. We were able to use picture books to critically analyze the grammar of visual design and examine ways in which printed text can work with and against images. The books selected were works of historical fiction, and they are all available from international distributors. We also used contemporary images from advertising to look at the effects of colour, angles, vectors, gaze, and spatial layout as described in Kress and van Leeuwen's "Grammar of visual design" (2001, in Lewis, D. *Reading contemporary picture books*). Elizabeth, a student from the gifted and talented program who was an accomplished writer, had never considered the use of images to persuade or affect the emotions of the reader. "Is that how it works?" she marvelled.

It was clear through an analysis of the picture books and the musical photo stories that the works of historical fiction required the best qualities of print, image, and sound. The digital images from the museum archives

Multimodal Picture Books

Title	Plot summary	Learning opportunities
The Lost Diamonds of Killie Crankie (Crew & Gouldthorpe, 1995)	Three young boys, in searching for rare topaz, unearth the story of the genocide of the Tasmanian aborigines.	Realistic use of photographs, letters, archival material, and scanned images to establish authenticity of the story.
The Mystery of Eileen Mor (Crew & Geddes, 2005),	A ghost story surrounding the disappearance of three lighthouse keepers.	Angles, vectors, gaze, and light used for dramatic effect. Sombre pictures enhance sparse language.
Quetta (Crew & Whatley, 2002)	The rescue and adoption of a shipwrecked child by a "suitable" member of the community.	The gaze of the rescuer demands empathy; the soft muted colours indicate the author's sympathies.
The Castaways of the Charles Eaton (Crew & Wilson, 2002)	Another Pacific shipwreck and rumours of the fate of the survivors.	Grim detail and dramatic use of colour. Research into archival and historical documents evident.

Figure 8.4. The texts above were read and critically analyzed.

established the authenticity of the settings and facts; sound recordings were used for atmosphere or narration; and the fictional story was recorded in print. In the photo stories where print was superimposed over the images, the text was hard to read. This type of print on images suited autobiographical and instructional photo stories with sparse text, but the historical fiction stories were too long to produce in this way.

We used Microsoft Office PowerPoint to create slides of the written narrative—the program allows writers to spell-check, edit, select fonts, and modify spatial layout. They determined the amount of text per slide by how long it took to read and how large it needed to be for easy reading onscreen. The slides were numbered, then saved individually as jpeg files. In Photo Story, the text pages were uploaded as jpeg files in the same way as images were integrated into the story sequence.

The construction of the photo story as a book-like reading experience allowed many fruitful discussions about reading and texts. Fellow students read the pages of text aloud so that the writer could adjust the timing for each page in tune with the rate at which people read. Slide transitions could be selected to resemble the turning of pages or cinema effects like fading and cuts. The use of the zoom function meant that not just the angles and vectors of the pictures could be manipulated but also the reading path that the reader's eyes were invited to follow. We discussed how people read screens as opposed to pages of print. Students had to make decisions about which words to emphasize as the camera zoomed. Choices of colour and font became important for the aesthetic experience being created. The social construction of meaning, through conversation with peers, was crucial in testing the work. Thus the acquisition of the vocabulary of multimodal design was necessary to formulate and articulate ideas.

It was difficult for some of the children to avoid the notion of making a movie—they wanted to find pictures that would act out the narrative. Multimodal texts allow us to create meaning using digital images and sounds from different contexts. Not all of these match or illustrate the actions of the characters; some extend or contest the narrative. These creative gaps and spaces are important for eliciting aesthetic responses. Wolfgang Isner identifies the characteristics of literature that stimulate creative participation in meaning making. His words are as true for reading as they are for writing, speaking, and viewing.

> Whenever the reader bridges the gaps, communication begins … the blanks leave open the connections between perspectives in the text, and so spur the reader into coordinating these perspectives—in other words they induce the reader to perform basic operations within the text. (Isner cited in Thomson 1987, 123)

There have to be gaps and intuitive leaps. We examined the way in which picture books sometimes leave gaps for the reader's imaginations. Many of the children said they preferred to imagine their favourite characters from literature and were often disappointed by movie adaptations. This is because most movies fill in the blanks, but multimodal texts can be created with spaces and absences that invite the viewer into a deeper interactivity with the story. This was achieved in a number of the photo stories because the digital images of places, objects, and settings did not disclose characters or actions—this was left to the written text.

Discoveries

The "learning by design" framework allowed for points of departure and return. The work was guided by the students' experiences and motivations, which led to some surprising new discoveries. Some elected to stay with linguistic literacies that they were most comfortable with whereas others expanded the task in new directions.

Maria travelled fourteen kilometres to the workshops from the family farm. Her grandmother drove her each week and stayed for part of the workshop. Maria's intention was to learn to use Photo Story, but she changed her original story in response to the museum collection. Although Maria's great-grandfather was a local Italian storekeeper, his story had not been part of the museum's migrant history collection. Maria's research reinvigorated the extended family's interest in old photos and oral accounts. As her grandmother said, when she went to school, she was not encouraged to discuss her Italian heritage. She marvelled at Maria's photo story and the way it was received and valued by the museum, school, and university.

When teachers permeate the boundary between the community and the school, we begin to rewrite the history of educational disadvantage for certain groups. We not only allow disempowered voices access to the discourse of education, as suggested by Gee (1996), but the interchanges alter the discourse.

The project concluded with the launch of the Cyberwriters CD-ROM by Australian children's author and illustrator, Rachel Tonkin. Rachel spoke to the children about her use of images and text in the creation of her recent award-winning picture book, *Leaf Litter*. The project was captured for pre-service teachers as a CD-ROM and is available on the Cyberwriters Project website.

The Cyberwriters project demonstrates that historical fiction can be created multimodally for and by the computer-literate generation of young people. The tasks encourage social construction of meaning, rich discussion, and authentic deep learning. Teachers and students now have free access to authoring tools and digital resources. These tools are user-friendly and require only an enquiring mind, a willingness to try something new, and perseverance — all of which are the qualities we expect of our students and which we can model. The old world is able to speak to the new as children and teachers make these creative connections together.

REFERENCES

Burrows, Peter, O. Clarke, K. Souminen, M. Kalantzis, and B. Cope. 2007. *Designing for learning: Integrating digital content into learning tasks*. NSW: Primary English Teachers Association.

Gee, James Paul. 1996. *Social linguistics and literacies: Ideology in discourses*, 2nd ed. Bristol PA: Taylor & Francis.

Kalantzis, Mary, B. Cope, and H. Fehring. 2002. *Multiliteracies: Teaching and learning in the new communications environment*. NSW: Primary English Teaching Association.

Healy, Annah. 2008. Expanding student capacities: Learning by design pedagogy. In: Healy Annah, ed., *Multiliteracies and diversity in education*. (2–29). South Melbourne AU: Oxford University Press.

Kress, Gunther and Theo van Leeuwen. 2001. Grammar of Visual Design. In: Lewis, David. *Reading contemporary picture books: Picturing text*. London: Routledge.

Mackey, Margaret. 2002. *Literacies across media: Playing the text*. London: Routledge.

Munns, Geoff, Leonie Arthur, and Toni Downes, et al. 2006. *Motivation and engagement of boys. Evidence-based teaching practices*. Canberra: Australian Government Department of Education, Science and Training.

Thomson, Jack. 1987. *Understanding teenagers' reading: Reading processes and the teaching of literature*. North Ryde: Methuen Australia.

Unsworth, Len, A. Thomas, A. Simpson, and J. Asha. 2005. *Children's literature and computer-based teaching.* Berkshire: Open University Press.

Unsworth, Len. 2006. *E-Literature for children: Enhancing digital literacy learning.* Oxon: Taylor & Francis Group/Routledge.

For access to the Cyberwriters Project website, email <jethompson@csu.edu.au>.

Chapter 9

Developing Agency and Voice: Radically Rewritten Traditional Tales

Heather Lotherington

Traditional children's stories are alive and well, embedded in the fabric of social communication. Reality television programs such as *Beauty and the Geek* and *The Bachelor* re-enact in contemporary guise the traditional narratives *Beauty and the Beast* and *Cinderella*. In the financial pages of *The Globe and Mail*, an analysis of income trusts is based on *The Three Little Pigs*—investments are categorized as built of straw (least stable), sticks (tentative durability), or bricks (solid). This financial analysis shares a space in my files beside other media accounts providing social commentary on new media (*Little Red Riding Hood* communicating with grandma on a cell phone), ecological warnings (no one sleeping in Mama bear's bed because of global warming), and advertising cars (three sizes of Hummer, one of which Goldilocks finds just right). These communications anticipate automatic recognition of traditional children's story characters, plots, settings, and lessons.

I discovered what a sample of Toronto's multicultural children knew about traditional stories in 2003, when I spent a sabbatical conducting ethnographic research at Joyce Public School (JPS), an inner-city elementary school in northwest Toronto. During this experience, I volunteered to help out in the school where needed. I soon found myself assisting in ESL classes and reading stories to kindergarten children who had been identified as at risk in emergent English literacy development due, mainly, to their language and cultural backgrounds. I had an enormous amount of fun reading to very young children, and was heartened to experience their growing familiarity with storybook reading, with English, and with the stories included in the little library corner of the kindergarten classroom. But I grew increasingly aware of the disconnect between the children whom I was reading to and the stories they most wanted to hear, like *Goldilocks and the Three Bears* which was a runaway favourite.

There was one child in the classroom who was Anglo-Canadian; the other children had backgrounds that circled the world, including cultures from Asia, the Caribbean, Europe, and South America. Many did not know English; some had no familiarity with storytelling generally; a few did not connect stories and books at all. In conversations with the principal, I suggested that we consider a research project to retell the popular stories through the children's eyes as a more inclusive approach to learning to read and write. The idea was that by rewriting the stories with a twist through the children's diverse linguistic and cultural vantage points, we could help them challenge the cultural exclusivity of the traditional narratives, while simultaneously gaining familiarity with them in tune with expected childhood education, and take ownership of their own emergent literacy learning. To do this, we would be reaching for Freire's critical literacy goal of writing the world as well as the word (Freire and Macedo 1987).

Multiliteracies at Joyce Public School

We began our journey by digitally retelling the story of *Goldilocks and the Three Bears*, the kindergarteners' favourite story, in grade 2 (chronicled in Lotherington and Chow 2006). Our theory-to-practice literacy research was inspired by the New London Group's stance that literacy education is out of sync with contemporary social needs; they exhort teachers and researchers to

> extend the idea and scope of literacy pedagogy to account for the context of our culturally and linguistically diverse and increasingly globalized societies, for the multifarious cultures that interrelate and the plurality of texts that circulate … [and] … for the burgeoning variety of text forms associated with information and multimedia technologies. (1996, 61)

Our collective goal was to develop approaches to literacy instruction focused on narrative learning that included language and literacy practices in our culturally diverse society, and to build opportunities for digital expression into literacy learning. We approached this mission through the teaching of traditional stories, an ancient and enduring educational medium.

The method we have developed is best described as "guided action research." We meet monthly for half-day teacher-researcher workshops, during which we talk about theory, technology, and each other's work; we plan narrative projects and trouble-shoot problems; we share emerging pedagogies and the children's work. The teachers are guided to create and conduct classroom projects that take place over the course of the school year in which children learn, retell, and rescript a well-known narrative using digital technologies and incorporating their language and cultural backgrounds in imaginative ways.

Building opportunities for developing voice and agency

The link between the oral and the written in emergent literacy is usually viewed as a linear development from learning to talk to learning to read and write. A decade before the Internet went public in the early 1990s, Walter Ong (1980) proposed a different relationship between literacy and orality. Focusing on television and radio, Ong talked about how we could not differentiate speech and writing so neatly in "a media-conscious world" where the public media provided a further layer of post-literate or *secondary* orality. The *primary* orality of child language acquisition leading to print literacy no longer adequately captured the sophisticated links between the world encoded on paper and the world re-encoded in electronic media.

This relationship is further complexified in contemporary times where media are now, at least partly, in the hands of the individual user. Kids in schools today are born into a digital generation that sees sophisticated miniaturized information and communication technologies that lead to a parallel virtual universe as a normal and natural part of life, just as their parents might have understood television, and their grandparents, radio. These new technologies introduce new ways of telling stories. Digital technologies open spaces for children to edit the stories that exist in print, adding their own imaginative touches as would have happened in oral story-telling before the era of print. With this idea in mind, we invite children to learn well-known stories that they will eventually inhabit as authors.

Voices in a multicultural society

Most of the children at JPS are speakers of languages other than English and French, and are at varied levels of learning English as a second language. We know from research that children are best positioned to learn a second language when instruction builds on the languages they know. However, given the remarkable range of languages in today's classrooms, it would be too difficult for one teacher to incorporate numerous home languages in literacy education when English is the language on the page.

The inclusion of multilingualism in our multiliteracies project is key to the idea of developing voice and agency. How does a child learn to express himself or herself in an appropriated school voice that is still being acquired in school? We wanted to make room for telling stories in more than one language and in more than one way. The stories could then be owned by the children. Furthermore, community members would have better access to children's school progress.

New ways of telling old stories: Children's inclusive retellings

Our project includes teachers of both primary and junior grades. In the planning stages of the project, we decided to focus on traditional children's literature. Teachers in primary grades have chosen to work with a traditional folk or fairy tale that thematically bridges curricular aims in the grade with which they are working (see Lotherington et al. 2008, for three primary teachers' narratives on this project). Stories from the traditional children's literature canon are favoured; narratives selected have included folk and fairy tales such as *The Three Little Pigs*, *The Three Billy Goats Gruff*, *Goldilocks and the Three Bears*, *The Gingerbread Man*, and *The Little Red Hen*; as well as fables, including *Chicken Little* and Aesop's fable *The Lion and the Mouse*. In the junior grades, teachers have worked with stories of a more international character that help children to understand life from a broader perspective, including a West African *Ananse* trickster tale and a traditional Chinese legend, *Mr Yu removes the mountain*.

Grade 2: The Little Red Hen

The Little Red Hen is a folk tale that teaches a lesson about the benefits of planning, hard work, and helping others. When the little red hen decides to bake bread and asks the barnyard animals to help her sow, harvest, and grind the wheat to bake bread, they all lazily decline. But after the hen has baked the bread, the barnyard animals want to eat it. In the traditional tale, the little red hen rejects their unearned interest in reaping the rewards of her labour, and eats the bread herself.

Sandra Chow decided to adapt *The Little Red Hen* in her grade 2 class, following her piloting of the rewritten *Goldilocks* stories in the first year of our study. Sandra had discovered in her grade 2 rewriting project that the changes in setting from the cottage in the woods to the bears' kitchen to their living room to their bedroom complicated the decisions the children had to make in order to reinterpret the setting and the characters through their own eyes. She chose *The Little Red Hen* as a fable with a clear moral lesson, which had a relatively simple setting that did not distract the children in their rescripting of the narrative as a contemporary story. The straightforward linearity of the fable helps students to understand narrative structure.

Figure 9.1. *The Little Red Hen* culturally reinterpreted and scripted as a play, with narrator, actors, scenery and musical interludes for scenery changes.

Sandra's aim was to make this timeless tale relevant to today's children. Her focus was on including children's sense of culture. We had discovered in the *Goldilocks* adaptations, that children understand very deeply the characters they create because they have to draw them in tune with their plotted narrative actions. We had also discovered that children's notions of culture included, very prominently, the digital world (Lotherington and Chow 2006).

The children had to reinterpret *The Little Red Hen* in a cultural context that made sense to them in terms of setting and foods. Through multiple readings—first of the canonical story, then different versions, including one with the little red hen making pizza, another in which she shares her food—and a careful progression of associated activities (for example, a comparison of versions using Venn diagrams, and storyboarding), we led the children to understand what a narrative is, and what this narrative tells us. Deciphering the essential narrative thread from the embellishments that contextualize it, as we have discovered in this story retelling research, is not easy. The children's mission was, then, to adapt the story slightly and with a great deal of guidance—to give them carte blanche would be to destroy the heart of the narrative, which must remain recognizable. This is a delicate adaptation.

The class discussed the ethical dimensions of the story, which gives the characters an opportunity to help a friend, and they brainstormed different possibilities and outcomes. Many children agreed that they would prefer to help out a friend who needed assistance in preparing food and then they could all share the prepared meal. Others chose the original ending, believing that it was fairer. The opportunity to adapt the characterization and then the ensuing actions to make sense within the amended story requires deep thinking about narrative structure and logical conclusions. It is interesting that, at grade 2, there was no consensus on the ending of the story, which indicates an educational climate of critical thinking and individual ownership over narrative decisions.

The children had to make the decisions that would frame their versions of the story: Who would be their characters? Where would these characters live? What food would they like to prepare? These decisions require coherence: a mermaid cannot make ice cream underwater, nor can a tiger in a zoo make a birthday cake.

The children developed personal versions of the story, choosing their settings, characters, and foods. In one interesting variation, the child chose to search out water in a desert with the help of her friends. After hearing everybody's versions, the class voted on their favourites, choosing a few that they could jointly dramatize. Once the most popular versions were selected, we grouped the children to collaboratively script one variation as a play, moving the narrative into a new genre.

In the children's selected revisions, the characters help the protagonist. The values of helpfulness, cooperation, and industriousness do not have to be relearned in these children's plays, where characters agree to contribute and, consequently, get to share the yummy results.

The contexts and characters of the children's adaptations tended to be fanciful—princesses in castles, wild animals in deserts, and creatures under the sea, echoing the media worlds children inhabit outside of school hours in television, movies, and video games. However, the food that children created in their plays reflected everyday foods such as hot dogs and instant packaged macaroni and cheese, and favourite treats like birthday cakes. The children researched their food preparation, brought in recipes and, in the process, transformed the little red hen's relatively simple original question "Who will help me plant this wheat?" into questions following the cooking instructions in cook books and on packages, and even using fractions as in "Who will help me add a half-cup of flour to the mixture?" The auxiliary reading done in researching how to make favourite foods invisibly accelerated the level of reading the children were doing. Recipes, including those in cook books, are written for an audience of competent readers, not 7-year-olds!

The children created the costumes and scene sets for each play, in keeping with their new contexts. They wrote the voices for actors and a narrator, and they performed their plays before a live audience of school children, taking care to arrange for short musical interludes while the sets were changed from play to play. The plays were videotaped and programmed, using iMovie to add a soundtrack to still pictures or video, which gave children a chance to do voice-overs (Figure 9.1). The availability of multiple soundtracks allows children to polish their performances; it also invites the possibility of multiple soundtracks in different languages, which can be added by teachers, educational assistants, or parents who volunteer to help.

Grade 5 Special Education: *Ananse's Feast*

Rhea Perreira-Foyle's grade 5 special education group created a beautiful animated bilingual story with a wonderful twist—the children retold a traditional Ananse (also spelled Anansi, Anancy) story in textbook English and the teacher created a Caribbean version.

Ananse, the trickster, is a traditional Ashanti character from West Africa who was brought to the Caribbean by African slaves. Ananse is a trickster spider who has to live by his wits, but is always getting into trouble. In the traditional story chosen by Rhea for her class, Ananse invites Crab to a dinner which Crab never gets to eat as he is continually told to wash his claws before he eats, which then get dirty again as he crawls back across the beach to Ananse's table. As Crab returns to wash his claws again and again, Ananse gobbles all the food. So Crab returns the favour and invites Ananse to eat at his table, which is under the sea. But Ananse, being a spider floats, and cannot dive down to Crab's dinner table, so he has to put rocks in his pockets to stay down. Naturally Crab insists, as did Ananse, on good table manners and Ananse is asked to take off his jacket. As Ananse floats helplessly to the surface, Crab finishes all the delicious food, just as Ananse had done when Crab was invited over.

In Rhea's grade 5 class, the children had varying special needs (including one child who had a mild intellectual disability), compounded by English being a second language or dialect so we were dealing with low levels of English literacy.

The children enjoyed the Ananse tale and, after learning the basic narrative, each rewrote the story based on a food from his or her cultural background. Two or three children made up completely new stories, but most rewrote *Ananse's Feast* as a "do unto others as you would have them do unto you" parable, through the eyes of their animal of choice eating a culturally familiar food.

Afterward, the class decided to turn the story into a movie, and they set out to create an animated video production. They selected one version of the children's stories that included rescripted narration and dialogue but retained the familiar characters. Rhea worked hard with the children to brainstorm the English words they would need to describe the crafty trickster Ananse and his mischievous actions. They had to construct a set for their story and design the clay figures that would represent the characters of Ananse and Crab. They made and painted a miniature cardboard scene set of a tropical beach in which the story could be re-enacted with the characters they had crafted from clay and art materials (Figure 9.2).

Using a digital camera to photograph each scene of their rescripted narration, including first the spider Ananse, then Crab, each greedily gulping their Plasticine food, the children created a linear series of photographs depicting the story action. To do this, the plot must be divided into photographable chunks, which requires a careful analysis of the story progression. The photos were uploaded to a computer and mounted in sequence in the movie-making program, iMovie, where they formed the basis for a beautiful claymation movie. The children then recorded the voice-overs for each segment, each child taping a scene in the English narrative voice that she or he had carefully developed with the teacher's help. Voice-over recording can be done using the built-in computer microphone in Apple laptops, but an inexpensive microphone can be used with computers that do not have a built-in microphone, and optionally with iMovie, too. As an added bonus, the teacher produced their beautifully photographed iMovie of *Ananse's Feast* as a DVD in two versions—the children's version in standard English followed by the teacher's re-narrated version of the children's iMovie in Caribbean English.

Figure 9.2. *Ananse* comes to life in clay

Rhea's story in two Englishes provides a solution to a delicate and educationally costly problem widely experienced in schools in the GTA. Many students of Caribbean backgrounds arrive in Toronto as fluent speakers of vernacular Caribbean-based creoles such as Jamaican Patwa (dialect spelling for *patois*) or Guyanese Creole, which is certainly understood, even if discouraged, in schools in their respective countries. When the children arrive in Canada, however, they may not realize that what they understand to be English is not understood as English in Canada. Teachers, similarly, are not sufficiently aware of creolized English varieties and may not have the expertise to help children see where there are differences in spoken and written varieties of English and where these differences might matter in communication. Many children, lacking help with English as a second dialect, have problems in English literacy that prevent them from succeeding in school. This is a sad injustice. Rhea's project offers an opportunity to explore different varieties of English in ways that are respectful of cultural differences, and can be used to illustrate Creole (oral) and English (written) diglossic usage. Furthermore, bringing traditional African Ananse stories into the classroom adds interest for those who have not met Ananse the trickster, while creating non-threatening familiar ground for those who have, and broadening everyone's education and amusement.

Conclusion

We set out to use traditional children's literature as a vehicle for story-rewriting in the classroom that would invite the backgrounds of multicultural children into the process of narrative learning. We brought into the Canadian classroom traditional narratives and world literature, and invited in community languages to complement English language learning. In this way, community bilingualism and multilingualism were welcomed as natural and normal, and home languages were seen as desired and useful media, not as inconvenient obstacles to the learning process. We invited contemporary digital story-telling devices and, in other class projects, comics and video games into developing pedagogies of story learning through story retelling and, in so doing, created spaces for children to try out their developing classroom voices beside the voices of more experienced storytellers, whose languages form a part of the larger community and the world we all inhabit. We did this through project-based learning centring on traditional children's literature.

The children participating in our research-driven story projects have provided feedback on the learning potential of project-based story-rewriting in a number of ways. Although our teacher-researcher collective does not subscribe to the limited paper-based conception of literacy embedded in the documents of the Education Quality and Accountability Office (EQAO) in Ontario, we have noted that the children's EQAO scores have improved. I do not attribute this improvement directly to particular action in our rewriting projects, but to the agency that such project-based learning builds into the children's literacy education. Developing and constructing imaginative, culturally-relevant narrative projects from traditional stories enables children to adventure into their own learning spheres, to relate the traditional to the contemporary, to develop critical literacy, and to search for new ways of expressing themselves. Using digital mediation to produce contemporary movies and presentations is highly motivating to children. Children learn to appreciate each other's work. Not only does a voting procedure, like the story favourites vote that Sandra instituted in her class, require children to critically review their peers' story lines but it also facilitates self-review by comparison.

Children also learn to work with each other. Story production is multidimensional and collaborative, requiring planning, multimodal orchestration, and the linking of learning and doing. Literacy development is understood to be multimodal and multidimensional. The final products, shared not just with class members but with other grades and parents in final year concerts, bring the widespread appreciation of community members. Finally, the children, themselves, have voiced their enjoyment in these projects, often asking whether they get to do something similar in the year following a project, or telling teachers long after the fact that they had a lot of fun writing the story they learned.

There is a place for children's literature front and centre in contemporary multiliteracies research leading to the development of children's voice and agency in the urban multicultural context. The traditional stories being learned and retold at JPS give the children enjoyment, agency, and an opportunity to develop their own voices in an emergent literacy project that reinforces both English, which so many children are acquiring, and home and community languages, which need support for the effective learning of ESL, and for respectful, successful multiculturalism.

REFERENCES

Freire, Paulo, with Donaldo Macedo. 1987. *Literacy: Reading the word and the world*. South Hadley, MA: Bergin and Garvey.

Lotherington, Heather and S. Chow. 2006. Rewriting *Goldilocks* in the urban, multicultural elementary school. *The Reading Teacher*, 60 (3), 244–252.

Lotherington, Heather, M. Holland, S. Sotoudeh, and M. Zentena. 2008. Teaching emergent multiliteracies at Joyce Public School: Three narratives of multilingual story-telling in the primary grades. *Canadian Modern Language Review*, 65 (1), 125–145.

New London Group. 1996. A pedagogy of multiliteracies: Designing social factors. *Harvard Educational Review*, 66 (1), 60–92.

Ong, Walter. 1980. Literacy and orality in our times. *Journal of communication*, 30 (1), 197–204.

Website

Mr Yu removes the mountain, a traditional Chinese legend, also known as *The foolish old man removes the mountain*s: <http://www.chinavista.com/experience/story/story3.html> (accessed March 27, 2009).

Thank you to my students in the graduate education course, Literacy and Social Context.

Section Four

Critical Reading of Print and Non-Print Texts

Chapter 10

Using Traditional and Multimodal Texts to Promote Multicultural Literacy and Intercultural Connections

Jamie Campbell Naidoo

> Now I know/now I see/through the gloom/many watch me/many slaves and many free/dark and light and in-between/all are praying/many voices/many languages/from Africa/and all the various/dialects of Spain/many voices/praying for me/so many voices/wishing me well, crying out/God be with you/hurry, hurry don't delay!/So many voices, joined as one/so many eyes in the gloom/seeing through darkness/watching me, singing out hopefully/as I escape!
> (Margarita Engle 2006, 171–2)

As she concludes the final stanza of Margarita Engle's *The Poet Slave of Cuba: A Biography in Poems of Juan Francisco Manzano*, an unnatural silence envelopes her grade 7 classroom. Ellen (all names are pseudonyms) is not surprised. Her students are mesmerized by this haunting collection of poems that describe the cruelties faced by slaves in Cuba. After a moment, Requain blurts out, "So he made it!" His comment is instantly followed by Kyanne's, "No he didn't! I bet they caught him." Maya, who has expressed a keen interest in the book's subject, remarks, "He had to make it. Otherwise, how would his poems have gotten published? I found a website with his poems. If he had been caught they wouldn't have been published. That old lady would have just trashed 'em after she killed him for running away." Picking up on Maya's cue, Ellen suggests that the class take a trip to the school library to research more about Juan Francisco Manzano and slavery in Cuba. She has already collaborated with the teacher-librarian to locate a list of useful Internet resources related to both topics.

A key website they are using with Ellen's students is that of the University of North Carolina at Chapel Hill, Documenting the American South (2001). This website contains an electronic version of *Poems by a Slave in the Island of Cuba, Recently Liberated*, an English translation of Manzano's poems, and a series of questions and answers related to slavery in Cuba. Ellen and the teacher-librarian have also created a WebQuest on Cuban slavery to guide students' online learning. In addition to working with electronic resources, students will locate both fiction and nonfiction books related to slavery in the American South or apartheid in South Africa. Students will use these books along with Cárdenas's award-winning international novel, *Old Dog* (2007), to construct background knowledge that will assist them as they develop a website that compares and contrasts slavery in the American South and in Cuba with apartheid in South Africa.

The above lesson is a rich example of incorporating multimodal learning with multicultural and international literature to facilitate intercultural understanding while engaging multiple new literacies. Students in Ellen's class are engaged in visual, auditory, and hands-on activities that require competency in multiple 21st-century literacies—information literacy, media literacy, web literacy, visual literacy, and cultural literacy. They are learning how to navigate new forms of traditional literacy strategies such as locating, evaluating, and synthesizing information in order to communicate on the Internet. At the same time, these students are reaching beyond the scope of their cultural experiences in Toronto to learn about historical events from the United States, Cuba, and South Africa. Ellen has purposefully selected a multicultural novel, *The Poet Slave of Cuba*, which has won several diversity awards for children's literature, including the Pura Belpré Award, the Américas Award, and the Children's and Young Adult's Book Award from the International Reading Association. She has also provided her students with copies of an international historical fiction novel, *Old Dog* by Teresa Cárdenas, which captures the raw emotions of slaves who were growing up on a sugar plantation in Cuba. These two books along with the Internet resources and students' self-selected texts provide a rich learning environment for examining the intersections of race, class, and culture in three diverse countries.

Student-generated knowledge from these resources can be applied to Canadian history to better understand the country's role in assisting runaway slaves and providing asylum for refugees. In turn, students may research their own family history to determine how their ancestors arrived in Canada. Considering the growing foreign-born and immigrant population in Canada, many students in Ellen's class may be recent immigrants with their own rich experiences that can be shared with their peers.

Multicultural literacy and intercultural connections

All children deserve to see accurate and positive representations of diverse cultures in the books they encounter. For children with diverse cultural backgrounds, positive images of their culture in children's literature assists with their ethnic identity development, provides positive role models, and supports richer connections with the text. For children outside the particular culture of their school, authentic and accurate literature about other cultures fosters acceptance of diversity, challenges stereotypes, and encourages stronger relationships with classmates from diverse cultural backgrounds.

Teachers and librarians serving in today's classrooms are charged with creating an open-forum for facilitating understanding and acceptance of diversity based upon culture, ethnicity, linguistic ability, religion, physical ability, immigration status, and sexual orientation. Schools are asked to become bridges between academic learning, students' home cultures, and world cultures. An excellent way to build these cultural bridges is to integrate culturally authentic and contemporary children's literature about diverse groups into the classroom to promote multicultural literacy, thereby introducing students to the cultures of fellow classmates, teachers, or future acquaintances. Educators should, however, go one step further than simply introducing different cultures through children's literature; rather, they should promote intercultural connections by inviting students to explore topics such as social justice, equality, and cultural authenticity. In doing so, they will provide students with an educational forum for exploring issues of race, class, and culture.

As the children they teach are becoming more tech-savvy, it is imperative that teachers become attuned to emerging technologies and the numerous ways to engage new literacies and to promote intercultural understanding of the diverse cultures prevalent in society. With each passing year, more children's books are published that exemplify "radical change" by defying tradition and using the new technologies to communicate cultural meaning through nonlinear organization and format, moving images, hypertext, and sound (Dresang 1999). These multimodal texts hold multiple layers of meaning and often possess a digital design with sidebars and other modes of communicating information through varied graphics, texts, and external websites. Multimodal books are highly desirable in new literacies classrooms where students currently use multiple modes of communication and information-seeking in their everyday encounters. The introduction of multimodal texts into the classroom, the library/resource centre, or other educational settings allows reluctant readers, English Language Learners (ELL), male students, and hands-on learners to discover new cultures through a format they may find more appealing or understandable.

A recent example of a multimodal, cultural picture book is Mora and López's (2007) *Yum!¡Mmmm!¡Qué rico!: Americas' Sproutings*. Throughout the text and illustrations of this vibrant picture book, children are exposed to multiple layers of meaning as they engage with two non-linear printed texts and multiple visual images. On the left-hand side of each two-page spread, an informational text describes the origins of various foods throughout North, Central, and South America (the Americas). The right-hand side of the double-page spread provides haiku celebrating various foods. Children have the opportunity to read the informational text only, the haiku only, or both. Their choice will influence the meaning that they take from the text. Through the informational texts, children will make intercultural connections as they realize that many of the foods they enjoy originate from other cultures. Children reading only the haiku will encounter onomatopoetic and alliterative words that will appeal to their senses as they are invited to "taste" the various foods. Read collectively, the informational text and haiku provide cultural facts and varied modes that inspire children to play with language.

The book's bold and blazing illustrations by Rafael Lopez virtually leap from the page, creating a visual fiesta. Vibrant painted images loaded with magical realism provide a sensory *celebración* in which children can almost taste the foods, feel the heat of the sun, and hear the squeals of delight as Papà eats a chili pepper. The illustrations are suffused with the colours and symbols of Latino cultures and refer to the art forms of Mexican folk art, naive art, and surrealism. Children poring over the illustrations can gain cultural meanings that are not discussed in the text.

The non-linear dual-texts in *Yum!¡MmMm! ¡Qué rico!: Americas' Sproutings* prepare students to read other non-linear texts found on websites such as menus and hyperlinks. The multiple layers of meaning found in both the text and illustrations prepare children to navigate through the visual and textual messages they will encounter simultaneously on the Internet. The cultural elements in both the text and illustrations encourage children to make intercultural connections between their culture and experiences with those cultures and experiences represented.

The following passage extends the idea of multimodal multicultural children's literature to include new literacies that are technology-enabled. It is through this concept that we can better understand how multicultural and international children's literature securely fits into new literacies classrooms.

Multicultural children's literature, new literacies, and technology

Emerging technologies are continuously changing the types of learning activities in contemporary classrooms, resulting in the need for new literacies to help children navigate multimodal texts. Fortunately, there are several ways for educators to incorporate new literacies and intercultural understanding into their children's literature program. These include

- moving fluidly in a two-way process between traditional and online multimodal texts
- utilizing Webquests
- engaging in social networking, web-publishing, and online collaborative projects
- creating websites demonstrating intercultural understanding through children's literature
- exploring digital books
  (Castek et al. 2006; Teclehaimanot and Lamb 2004)

Each of these methods will be discussed below along with classroom examples.

Fluid movement from traditional and online multimodal texts

High quality children's literature is a catalyst for new learning with new technologies. Children use multicultural and international literature as background information about a specific cultural group and then navigate to the Internet to research the topic further, to watch video clips, to chat with students from schools in different regions, and so on. Using the new knowledge and schemata created through these interactions, children then go back to traditional print multicultural or international literature to develop an even better understanding of the culture being explored. The interaction between traditional print texts and online multimodal texts is a two-way process where children use newly created meaning from one source to gain a richer comprehension of the information in the other source. Children can then use this new information to create their own online multimodal texts—digital books, websites, Wikipedia entries, and similar new tech items—that become part of the shared knowledge of the classroom.

In addition to the lesson on Cuban slavery that opened this chapter, an example of this two-way process can be found in the picture book *Los Gatos Black on Halloween* by Montes and Morales (2006). In it, readers are introduced to both Halloween and Dia de los Muertos (the Day of the Dead) through snappy rhymes sprinkled with Spanish phrases. Along with learning about the two holidays, children encounter many Spanish words whose meaning can be deciphered using contextual clues. But it is the spooky illustrations that ultimately lead readers of this book to online multimodal resources and engage them in new literacies. Lurking in many of the illustrations are ghosts and spirits that represent important characters from Mexican history and folklore. These cultural and historical allusions include Sor Juana Ines, Señora de las iguanas, La Planchada, and Diego Rivera.

When children first read this book, they may not notice these characters if they are unfamiliar with Mexican culture. With guidance from an astute teacher or teacher-librarian, children can be directed toward the Internet to gain background information on them, then return to the book to develop a richer understanding. Perhaps then they might return to the Internet to create their own multimodal texts, perhaps a Wikipedia article on the Latino historical references in the book or they may go to the illustrator's webpage and print masks of these characters. Children could use the masks to dramatize portions of the text, incorporating supplemental information about the two holidays and the historical and cultural illusions. They could record their performances on video and upload them on the StoryTubes project on YouTube to share with other children around the world.

In an elementary school in Alabama, children in a grade 2 class read *Los gatos black on Halloween*, created masks that they downloaded from the illustrator's website, and then used the state's free virtual reference library to search an online encyclopedia for elementary school children in order to locate additional information on Day of the Dead customs, particularly the significance of candy sugar skulls. Using information from this resource, students created candy skulls to honour a pet that had died. Figure 10.1 shows one of the students using Yuyi Morales's website to learn more about the illustrations and historical figures.

Figure 10.1. A grade 2 student uses the illustrator Yuyi Morales's website to download character masks.

Through activities such as these, children have an opportunity to experience the two-way flow between traditional and multimodal texts and to make intercultural connections between their own culture and that of the Latin American countries represented in the books. At the same time, the children would be engaging their knowledge of new literacies—visual literacy (to understand the historical and cultural allusions), web literacy (to navigate the Internet), informational literacy (to determine acceptable sources of information), cultural literacy (to understand the significance of the allusions to Latino cultures), and technology literacy (to create a Wikipedia article or YouTube video).

Webquests

Educators can also create literature-based webquests to facilitate multicultural literacy and intercultural connections using both multimodal and traditional print children's literature. Webquests are inquiry-based approaches that "provide an authentic, technology-rich environment for problem solving, information processing, and collaboration.... [They] center the experience on reading by using books as the focal point for activities" to explore theme, character, and plot (Teclehaimanot and Lamb 2004). If a teacher were to create a webquest based on a novel like Deborah Ellis's *Sacred Leaf* (2007), he or she could create questions requiring higher-order thinking related to the book's setting (Bolivia), topic (Cocalero farmers and the coco industry), and plot (effects of the illegal drug cocaine on Cocalero farmers). Either while reading the novel or after reading the novel, students could use a teacher-generated webquest to learn more, using new literacies and developing their intercultural understanding of Bolivians. An excellent resource for locating examples of webquests is Annette Lamb's (2007) "Literature-based WebQuests" designed for different levels, kindergarten through high school, which sets out the criteria to consider when evaluating or creating your own webquest.

As an extension of the books she has used with her grade 2 students (Montes 2006) and with her grade 5 students (Canales 2005), a teacher-librarian in South Carolina engaged both student groups to collaboratively complete a Day of the Dead webquest <http://its.guilford.k12.nc.us/webquests/dayofdead/dodead.htm>. By working together on the webquest, the older students were able to share their skills at navigating the web and their skills in information literacy with their younger counterparts, allowing the grade 2 students to evaluate information about the celebration that they might not be able to find on their own. At the same time, this collaboration allowed both student groups to learn more about the celebration while making deeper connections with the Mexican cultures represented in the books being read.

Online collaborative projects and social networking

Students can work with their classmates from other countries to better understand one another's cultures, using websites such as Kids' Space, Kidscribe! <http://www.brightinvisiblegreen.com/kidscribe/>, and Bookhooks <http://www.bookhooks.com/note.cfm> where students write their own texts about their cultures; using social networking environments such as wikis and blogs; and through traditional sources such as email or chat. A plethora of websites exist that allow tweens and teens to blog about their favourite books. Teen readers from different schools or communities could blog about their reactions to books like *Sacred Leaf* while addressing issues of race, class, and culture. Classroom teachers could work with teachers from other school systems, perhaps in another province, and have students from other systems blog their responses to the books in a teacher-created book blog or discussion forum. The website ePals <http://www.epals.com/> also provides ways for teachers and students to connect with other classrooms around the world. Books like *Sacred Leaf* open up new windows on the lives of children in Bolivia. After researching the location of Bolivia and gathering other information about the country, Canadian students will have familiarized themselves enough to benefit from contact with students from schools in Bolivia or to even by starting inquiry projects to benefit street children in Bolivia or in their own community.

Creating websites

Another example of how students can use children's literature and multimodal texts that promote intercultural understandings is the website "Breaking Down Walls." Grades 4 and 5 students in Wisconsin created the website in the ThinkQuest library <http://library.thinkquest.org/CR0212302/index.html>, which describes the importance of learning about and accepting cultures that are different from one's own. It includes an example of using children's literature to learn about diversity and a PowerPoint presentation related to acceptance. Students begin by reading international or multicultural literature about a particular culture, navigate online to learn more about the culture and to connect with students from that culture, and then they create a website that provides opportunities for other students to learn about cultural acceptance. The interaction with students from other cultures helps to foster their sense of intercultural connections and understanding.

Exploring digital books

Exploring digital books, particularly digital picture books, is a further way to integrate multicultural and international children's literature into the new literacies classroom to cultivate intercultural understanding. Castek, Bevans-Mangelson, and Goldstone (2006) assert that digital picture books "build students' understanding of story structures and introduce new opportunities to develop online navigational skills" (717). By using digital picture books, teachers and teacher-librarians are able to easily supplement their physical book collection with multicultural and international titles that might not otherwise be readily accessible.

Numerous for-profit and not-for-profit resources are available that contain a varied range of multicultural and international digital books. Some of the more notable ones are Lookybook, TumbleBooks, One More Story, International Children's Digital Library, and Digital Gallery of World Picturebooks. Each of these sources contains digital books that can encourage children's increasing intercultural understanding and their ability to incorporate new literacies.

Lookybook <http://www.lookybook.com/> contains complete electronic copies of all types of picture books, including those celebrating diverse cultures. Located on this free website is a Lookybook version of Morales' (2003) *Just a minute,* which could be read by children to introduce *Dia de los*

Muertos and a discussion of the significance of death in the Mexican culture. Children could compare this book with other books about Latino cultures, for example, Elya and Salerno's (2006) *Bebé goes shopping*, available in digital book format from TumbleBooks <http://www.tumblebooks.com/>. Although Lookybook is free, TumbleBooks is available only by subscription. However, Tumblebooks does include animation and sound in contrast to the static nature of Lookybooks.

Keeping with our theme of books about the Latino cultures, children could view Carling's (1998) *Mama and papa have a store* or Flores Scaramutti de Naveda, McDonald, and López's (2002) *Juancito siempre valiente/Brave Little Juan* on the International Children's Digital Library. This free collection of books contains digital copies of children's picture books from around the world and about many diverse cultures.

Another collection of international children's picture books is the Digital Gallery of World Picture Books, a free collection that provides an opportunity for children to view picture books from Japan and older books from the West but published from the 18th century to the 1930s. Children could use these books to learn about the social climate of countries around the world during a particular historical period.

One final source of digital picture books is One More Story, a subscription-based collection of books with both animation and sound. An example of an international book about a culture that differs from Canadian or American cultures is Léonard and Prigent's (2002) *Tibili: The little boy who didn't want to go to school*. This story, originally published in France, describes a little boy in Africa who does not want to go to school. Children could read this digital book and compare it with other digital books about specific African cultures, available from any of the aforementioned resources.

Qualities	• Free of stereotypes • Provide just enough information to help students use new literacies to navigate and find additional information • Possess integrity and authenticity • Exhibit some of the radical change qualities described by Dresang (1999)
Locating	• United States Board on Books for Young People (USBBY) Outstanding International Booklists <http://www.usbby.org/> • U.S. book awards celebrating cultural diversity (the Asian Pacific Islander, Pura Belpré, Américas, and Coretta Scott King awards to name a few) <http://www.pages.drexel.edu/~dea22/multaward.htm> • Literary awards that celebrate the best children's literature from each country, such as books recommended by IBBY Canada <http://www.acs.ucalgary.ca/~dkbrown/awards.html>

Figure 10.2. Identifying exemplary international and multicultural books

Books are windows into the soul of a society, illuminating the social, political, and cultural mores that underlie different worlds. It is through the illustrations and texts of books that children encounter these messages and discern the dominant culture's view toward other cultural groups.

Connecting multicultural and international children's literature with new literacies through the new technologies empowers teachers to explore issues of class, race, and culture with their students. Children generally display a high propensity toward the adoption of new technologies. When teachers use these vehicles to promote cultural understanding, the level of their students' success is significantly enhanced and they feel empowered to make intercultural connections that will last the rest of their lives.

REFERENCES

Castek, Jill., Jessica Bevans-Mangelson, and Bette Goldstone. 2006. Reading adventures online: Five ways to introduce the new literacies of the Internet through children's literature. *Reading Teacher*, 59 (7), 714–728.

Dresang, Eliza T. 1999. *Radical change: Books for youth in a digital age.* New York: H.W. Wilson.

International Reading Association. 2001. Integrating literacy and technology in the curriculum. <http://www.reading.org/General/AboutIRA/PositionStatements/TechnologyPosition.aspx> (accessed March 27, 2009).

New London Group. 1996. A pedagogy of multiliteracies: Designing social futures. Harvard Education Review, 66 (1). Available from <http://wwwstatic.kern.org/filer/blogWrite44ManilaWebsite/paul/articles/A_Pedagogy_of_Multiliteracies_Designing_Social_Futures.htm> (accessed March 27, 2009).

Teclehaimanot, Berhane and Annette Lamb. 2004. Reading, technology, and inquiry-based learning through literature-rich webquests. From *Reading Online*, 7 (4). <http://www.readingonline.org/articles/teclehaimanot/> (accessed March 27, 2009).

RESOURCES

Children's books and websites

Bookhooks <http://www.bookhooks.com/note.cfm> (accessed March 27, 2009).

Canales, Viola. 2005. *The Tequila Worm.* New York: Random House.

Cárdenas, Teresa. 2007. *Old dog.* Toronto: Groundwood Books.

Carling, Amelia Lau. 1998. *Mama and papa have a store.* New York: Dial Books.

Digital Gallery of World Picture Books: <http://www.kodomo.go.jp/gallery/index_e.html> (accessed March 27, 2009).

Ellis, Deborah. 2007. *Sacred Leaf.* Toronto: Groundwood Books.

Elya, Susan M. and Steven Salerno. 2006. *Bebé goes shopping*. New York: Harcourt.

Engle, Margarita. 2006. *The poet slave of Cuba: A biography of Juan Francisco Manzano*. New York: Henry Holt.

Flores Scaramutti de Naveda, Carlota, E. McDonald, and H. López. 2002. *Juancito siemprevaliente/Brave little Juan*. Lima, Peru: Biblioteca Nacional del Perú/National Library of Peru.

Hoad-Reddick, Adrian. BookHooks: Publish illustrated book reports online. <http://www.bookhooks.com/note.cfm> (accessed March 27, 2009).

International Children's Digital Library: <http://www.icdlbooks.org/> (accessed March 27, 2009).

Kids' Space Foundation. Kids' Space: Of kids, by kids, for kids. <http://www.kids-space.org/>, (accessed March 27, 2009).

Kidscribe! <http://www.brightinvisiblegreen.com/kidscribe/> (accessed March 27, 2009).

Lamb, Annette. Literature learning ladders: Literature-based WebQuests. <http://eduscapes.com/ladders/themes/webquests.htm> (accessed March 27, 2009).

Léonard, Marie and André Prigent. 2002. *Tibili: The little boy who didn't want to go to school*. La Jolla, CA: Kane/Miller Book Publishers.

Lookybook: <http://www.lookybook.com/> (accessed March 27, 2009).

Montes, Marisa and Yuyi Morales. 2006. *Los gatos black on Halloween*. New York: Henry Holt.

Mora, Pat and Rafael López. 2007. *Yum!¡Mmmm! ¡qué rico!: Americas' Sproutings*. New York: Lee & Low Books.

Morales, Yuyi. 2003. *Just a minute: A trickster tale and counting book*. San Francisco, CA: Chronicle Books.

Morales, Yuyi. 2008. *Los gatos black on Halloween*. from <http://www.yuyimorales.com/gatosblack/gatos_black.html> (accessed March 27, 2009).

One More Story: <http://www.onemorestory.com/> (accessed March 27, 2009).

StoryTubes project on YouTube <http://www.storytubes.info/> (accessed March 27, 2009).

University of North Carolina at Chapel Hill. 2001. *Poems by a slave in the island of Cuba, recently liberated*; translated from the Spanish, by R. R. Madden, M.D. with the history of the early life of the negro poet, written by himself; to which are prefixed two pieces descriptive of Cuban slavery and the slave-traffic, by R. R. M. Electronic edition from Documenting the American South: <http://docsouth.unc.edu/neh/manzano/manzano.html> (accessed March 27, 2009).

WebQuests: Day of the Dead webquest: <http://its.guilford.k12.nc.us/webquests/dayofdead/dodead.htm> (accessed March 27, 2009).

Chapter 11

The Lion, the Witch, and the Cereal Box: Reading Children's Literature across Multimedia Franchises
Naomi Hamer

The tween age group, namely preadolescents between the ages of 8 and 12, constitute a heavily targeted niche for the branding and cross-marketing of products. Consequently, books aimed at tween readers are often part of multimedia franchises that may include film and television adaptations, affiliated music albums, online fan clubs, video games, clothing, and cosmetics. Moreover, digital technologies and cultures have become central to how tween readers engage with books. Preadolescent readers frequently use websites, chat rooms, and other online forums for discussion and reflection on books, particularly those that are linked to popular franchises.

In light of these trends, contemporary tween books and their preadolescent readers require teachers to use innovative approaches for literacy education that take into account consumer and digital cultures. This chapter will explore several ways that multimedia adaptations and franchised products may provide opportunities for teachers and students to critically engage with children's literature.

The transformation of Narnia

The recent film adaptation of C.S. Lewis's *The Chronicles of Narnia: The Lion, the Witch and the Wardrobe* (2005) provides a key example of contemporary children's book publishing as a cross-media phenomenon. Long considered a classic of English language children's literature, the Narnia book series has been adapted a number of times since its original publication in 1950, including incarnations as a theatrical production, an animated feature (1979), a radio play, and twice as a BBC television serial (1966, 1989). However, the December 2005 release of the Disney/Walden Media film adaptation and its related multimedia franchise remodelled the text dramatically to situate it within post-Harry Potter media culture. The book is now part of an extensive franchise that includes DVDs, collectible products, merchandise, video games, and interactive websites. The total worldwide box office revenue was cited as $744,783,957, making it the 20th-highest-grossing movie of all time (Worldwide grosses, Box Office Mojo). The DVD was released in April 2006 in the UK, North America, and Europe. This franchise will be expanded further with the release of adaptations of the sequels *Prince Caspian* in May 2008 and *The Voyage of the Dawn Treader* in May 2010.

Narnia's current status as a multimedia phenomenon, rather than an isolated literature text, requires teachers to explicitly address the multimedia and commercial aspects of texts. During fieldwork in a grade 3 class in Toronto, Canada (2005–2006), I worked closely with the classroom teacher to organize a series of literacy activities and informal group discussions concentrated on a range of Narnia texts.[1] Framed by these classroom experiences with Narnia, I will give examples of how teachers may draw on children's literature as a multimedia phenomenon through

1. using old and new media adaptations, associated websites, and franchised products in conjunction with print texts
2. connecting extra-curricular media knowledge and experiences with school-based literacies in the classroom context
3. providing opportunities for young readers to respond to texts through the use of digital media and fan cultures

1. Using old and new media adaptations, associated websites, and franchised products in conjunction with print texts

A range of media texts and merchandise both within and outside the recent Narnia film franchise were used in my classroom fieldwork to initiate focus group discussions as well as creative and critical responses to the texts. Literacy activities around Narnia included children's picture book adaptations, older and current editions of the novels, the DVD of the film with special features, the Narnia.com website, the videogame, behind-the-scenes trivia books, board games, promotional advertisements for the film, collectible movie tie-in books found in breakfast cereal boxes, and re-releases of older adaptations.

---

[1] All transcript material in this chapter is taken from fieldwork data gathered in 2005-2006 in Toronto, Canada, as part of doctoral research for my PhD thesis, Institute of Education, University of London, United Kingdom [thesis to be submitted in 2009].

One innovative way to critically examine this range of cross-media adaptations, particularly those that are commercially situated, is for students to begin to examine the texts in terms of both *what* the scene is depicting and *how* the scene and the book and the film website are *designed* to be read and consumed by readers and viewers. Recent book design aimed at young readers strongly reflects changes in the production of these texts as part of multimedia franchises. As such, the books are designed not only in terms of what the written text is representing but also in terms of how the book fits into the broader meanings of a brand, franchise, or genre. Design in books for tween readers often exemplifies the influence of visual modes associated with popular culture, specifically advertising. Thus, the design of the texts also addresses the reader as not only an implied reader of the text but also a potential consumer of other products in a franchise, often linking products through repetition. The majority of young readers have already had many experiences with the branding and marketing of multimedia franchises. The literacy exercise at hand is not to teach students about branding and marketing but rather for them to critically examine how texts may be designed to both *represent* certain concepts that may be associated with a brand and to *address* certain readers and viewers.

Starter discussion questions on Narnia across the media

Below are some examples of preliminary questions that I used to lead discussion around cross-media *Narnia* texts. These discussion questions may serve as an introduction for a critical analysis activity, outlined in the following section. My discussion questions may be divided as:
   a. Questions about the representation across different media adaptations
   b. Questions about how the texts address different readers and viewers
   c. Questions that relate to the media preferences of the students

a. Questions about the representation across different media adaptations
- What are some of the differences between the adaptations? Different points of view? Character? Setting? Special effects? Which did you like better? Why?
- Is Lucy (and/or other siblings) the same as in the book? How is she different in the different interpretations? Did you imagine pictures in your head that are different from the characters in the TV version or in your head? Does it matter if the character is different from the book?

b. Questions about how the texts address different readers and viewers
- What do you think of the different covers? Can you tell from the cover if you will like this book? What can tell you tell from the cover about the story inside? When I was reading this book, I only knew this one cover. Does it matter if it has the film characters on the cover? If there is a photograph on the cover?

- From the cover how do you know who would read this book? What age group? For girls and boys? Is this a film/book that both girls and boys would like? Would someone older or younger than you like this book/movie? Would boys like the movie better?

c. **Questions that relate to the media preferences of the students**
- Does it make a difference if you see the film first? Would you usually watch the film/TV show or read the book? What do you prefer? Why (visual qualities, etc.)?
- What is the most important part of all the Narnia products for you? Do you like the books best? The movie? The game? The website? The characters? The pictures? The stories? The toys? Why?

Cross-media comparison activity with *Lucy through the Wardrobe*

A specific focus in discussion groups on representations of the same scene or character across different texts may help direct critical and comparative discussion of multimedia adaptations. In small groups of four or five students, we compared the same scene "Lucy through the Wardrobe" across the media adaptations. A scene comparison activity might include:
- "Lucy through the Wardrobe" in the original novel (1950)
- BBC television live action serial adaptation (1989)
- Walden Media/Disney feature film (2005)
- Movie tie-in book *Lucy's Adventure: The Quest for Aslan the Great Lion* (2005).

Comparing the novel and the feature film

The segment takes place in the first chapter of the original written text, and a number of narrative events occur, most significantly Lucy's first discovery of the wardrobe as a magic portal into Narnia (Lewis 1950, 6-10). In the original text the segment is written as follows:

> But instead of feeling the hard smooth wood of the floor of the wardrobe, she felt something soft and powdery and extremely cold. "This is very queer," she said, and went on a step or two further. Next moment she found that what was rubbing against her face and hands was no longer soft fur but something hard and rough and even prickly. "Why, it is just like branches of trees!" exclaimed Lucy. And then she saw that there was a light ahead of her; not a few inches away where the back of the wardrobe ought to have been, but a long way off (Lewis 1950, 8).

This scene may be read together in small groups or by the teacher to the whole class, followed by the viewing of the same episode in the recent feature film. The scene leading up to the wardrobe scene in the feature film is quite distinct from the written text as the exploration of the house has been transposed to a game of hide-and-seek. This upbeat pacing is enhanced by the soundtrack that includes the song "Oh, Johnny," an American dance music hit from the 1940s. The entry of Lucy into the room with the wardrobe begins silently. As she removes the sheet from the wardrobe, mysterious music plays and a close-up shot of Lucy's face reveals her delighted expression. An aerial shot represents Lucy as she moves through the wardrobe backwards, hitting the trees and turning to find herself in snowy forest. The fantastical element of the moment is enhanced by crescendo in the music and the audible crunchiness of snow.

Comparing with an older adaptation, the BBC television serial

A comparison of the same scene as represented in the BBC television adaptation provides many differences with the current film adaptation to draw attention to media production choices in discussion of the scene. The pacing of the BBC television serial follows the pacing of the original text. When Lucy enters the wardrobe, the camera jumps to a close-up shot of Lucy's face surrounded by fur coats. "How funny" Lucy says, slowly putting on a coat and walking into the snow. There is then a shot with the perspective from above the lamppost down at Lucy. The music used in the scene involves orchestral sounds of flutes, trumpets, and violins echoing each other, but with no specific crescendo when Lucy enters the fantasy world.

Using the movie tie-in book *Lucy's Adventure*

Following the viewing of "Lucy through the wardrobe" in the feature film, the same scene may be read in the movie tie-in book *Lucy's Adventure: The Quest for Aslan, the Great Lion* (2005), one of four collectible movie tie-in books released in the lead-up to the film and distributed in the UK as gifts in breakfast cereal boxes. Each of these movie tie-in books distinctly follows the narrative from the point of view of one child protagonist. Following the action of the film, the written text of the movie tie-in book illustrates slightly different pacing, tone, and point of view than in the original text.

> Inside, it was dark and surprisingly cold, as if there was a wind. Lucy decided to hide deep among the coats, so she put out her hand to feel for the back of the wardrobe. It seemed to be a very big wardrobe and Lucy had to really stretch and stretch and then she felt something…"Ouch!" Lucy frowned. That was strange—she had touched something prickly. Why would there be something prickly in the wardrobe? She took a step forward. Crunch. (*Lucy's Adventure*, 7–8).

A comparison between the original novel and this tie-in text may enhance discussions with students about how a story may change in the adaptation from novel to film to movie merchandise. In addition, these tie-in texts exemplify the new role of Narnia, serving as books to read but also as collectible items related to a greater franchise. Thus, they may provide the opportunity for teachers and students to discuss why free collectible books may be produced as promotional advertisements for an upcoming film.

Cross-Media Analysis Chart

	Original Novel	Disney Film	*Lucy's Tie-in* Book	BBC Serial
Modes Which modes are used in this scene—audio, film, written language and so on?				
Representational Who or what are the important characters/settings/objects in this scene? What do they represent in the story as a whole?				
Interpersonal Whose point of view is the story told from? How? Who is the targeted viewer/reader?				
Compositional How is the scene composed? What is the central image in the scene? How are certain parts of the scene given more significance?				
Medium (Book, DVD, Television) What special features does the type of medium bring to the scene?				

Figure 11.1.

Following engagement with and preliminary discussion of these cross-media texts, this analysis chart (Figure 11.1) may be used to examine how different media production and design elements work together to represent a scene. This chart may be used by a teacher in a class lesson, individually by students, or in small-group work. Analysis categories used in this chart are derived from Kress and van Leeuwen's theory of multimodality (2001), and from the analytical framework proposed by Burn and Parker (2003), particularly in their analysis of educational websites.[2]

2. Connecting extra-curricular media knowledge and experiences with school-based literacies in the classroom context

In another focus group, I engaged with students in a comparison of a scene across adaptations with the four siblings entering Aslan's camp with the beavers and other mythological creatures. The earlier BBC adaptation *The Chronicles of Narnia: The Lion, the Witch, and the Wardrobe* (1988–89) triggered harsh critical judgments from the grade 3 students who evaluated older adaptations, drawing on their knowledge of and experience with contemporary special effects and costuming.

> J: The bowl is like plastic. The sword looks like plastic.
> V: Be quiet.
> J: We are getting bored now.
> S: It's okay. It's not bad. It's pretty good for like the 1980s.
> P: 1980s.
> C: 1989.
> S: Oh that's Mr...That's the beavers?!
> Yeah.
> P: They're mutated.
> C: Cool.
> V: It's someone in a costume.
> They're mutated.
> S: It's pretty good costumes for...
> J: Look at the little elves. They are so cute.
> S: Victor. The costumes are really good for the 1980s.
> C: Or 1990s.
> They sort of look like toys.
> P: Why do they look like toys.
> C: Is that Peter?
> J: Peter. They look like grade four I think.
> S: Edmund looks older than Peter.

---

[2] The worksheets and analysis charts included in this chapter should be viewed as guides for discussion and activities. These resources may be adapted depending on age of participants, learning objectives, and the size of the group.

These students' critiques of the BBC adaptation of Narnia illustrate the great importance of authentic visual effects for these preadolescents who are experienced viewers of current film adaptations and their innovative applications of technology to create fantasy worlds. However, the discussion also reflects an assessment of casting (e.g., Edmund, the younger brother, looks older than Peter) that takes into account knowledge about characterization in the original text as well as the newer film. In addition, the dialogue between participants around how the costumes should be judged according to the time and context (the 1980s) of production exemplifies how cross-media adaptations may provide opportunities for preadolescents to bring their recreational media knowledge from outside the classroom to school contexts.

Livingstone's empirical study in the UK observed that young people "construct diverse lifestyles from a mix of different media" (Livingstone 2002, 15). Young readers may interact with texts in a way that involves *playing* with and across texts rather than traditional notions of literacy learning and reading. Mackey has coined the phrase "playing the text" to explore the ideas of how reading books and engaging with other types of media may illustrate different kinds of literacies (Mackey 2002). There is great potential for teachers to draw on this kind of cross-media play with a variety of texts. The use of cross-media adaptations, DVD bonus features, related fan videos, and website links may allow students to engage enthusiastically and critically with print and digital texts in the primary classroom.

Using bonus features and behind-the-scenes information

Many of the responses of the students during our discussions directly addressed the differences in representation between the new film and the older television adaptation. Some responses in the focus groups, for example, observe these differences explicitly: "she went in the wardrobe differently" "they didn't play hide and seek" "she's opening the door." However, as I will explore in the following section, the majority of the responses during the viewing of the BBC text also focused on aspects related to the representation itself, i.e., the set, special effects, costumes, and physical attributes of the actors.

The bonus features on a DVD or franchise website often contribute an additional level of engagement for viewers, including music videos, bloopers, behind-the-scenes featurettes, and trivia games. Many elements of these bonus features are continued through official websites, and online fan sites that may include fan-produced videos, photos, and written texts.

Bonus features and audio commentary about directorial and production decisions for the "Lucy through the wardrobe scene" provide an excellent starting point to discuss with students the adaptation of a scene from written text to film. For example, the DVD audio commentary for the film, the director, Adamson explains the changes in the adaptation from the book to film.

> Originally in the book Lucy actually discovers the wardrobe or steps into the wardrobe on their very first exploration of the house. And I sort felt when it came to doing that cinematically it didn't make as much sense that she finds it that way initially and goes back there playing hide and seek. I thought it made more sense if we actually started with the children bored not knowing what to do on a rainy day…and actually finding the wardrobe as a hiding place. And it made a lot more sense that she would then step into it. She wouldn't I didn't think logically if she just found the wardrobe she would naturally step in. But if she was hiding from her brothers. It was a more logical thing to do (Adamson *Chronicles*, DVD audio commentary).

A discussion that examines this commentary—alongside a viewing of the BBC and Disney/Walden Media representations of this scene—could lead into a number of activities where students could rewrite their own versions of the scene and ultimately stage the scene for a student-produced digital video or theatre production in the classroom.

Going beyond the DVD special features and audio commentary as starting points for discussion about media production, Ian Brodie's *Cameras in Narnia* (2005) and Perry Moore's *Official Illustrated Movie Companion* (2005) include costume design, workshop sketches for animation development, blueprints for set construction, and casting notes that may be used by individuals and groups to write, perform, or digitally record their own behind-the-scenes reports to present to other students.

Reviews of official website: narnia.com

Students also may share their extra-curricular media knowledge and experience through their critique of the official website, and other fan sites related to books and the adaptations. The Website Review Worksheet (Figure 11.2) structures their assessment of the official website of the film (narnia.com) and other favourite sites related to books in our discussions. The worksheet includes three statements and five categories to guide the website critique.

Many responses from the students reflect critiques rooted in *personal preferences as website users*.

> "It would be nice for funner games."
> "It has nothing to do for kids."
> "I liked when there were book and games and stuff"

Other responses illustrate *critical assessment of technical elements and choices of digital media production*.

> "I like how it looks 3-D."
> "The background is too dark"
> "Fast loading times—good. Game didn't work—bad. Add more photos—add"

Website Review Worksheet

Website Name: _____ Website Type: _____

(e.g., fan site, official franchise site, commercial site)

	What I like…	What I don't like…	What I would change / add…
Technical, Media Technology			
Fun, entertainment			
Educational, learning, information			
Media or modal choices (audio, video, photos, games)			
Story, characters, settings, themes, genre			

Figure 11.2.

The categories for review on the worksheet should guide and encourage the articulation of *personal preferences supported by assessment of the media production elements* of the website.

For example, one student wrote:

> "I liked the music because it makes me calm. I didn't like it when I couldn't play games. I will put some [bloopers] in the [website]." "Disney.com" was the best website in the whole wide world because "it has all the things I like. Example: Games, other sites, and they change games every month."

Overall the students' responses often highlighted the technical aspects of the website as well as the multimodal elements such as the music and visual background. This type of critical activity encourages attention to these non-narrative and media production elements of different texts, moving past the traditional focus on characters, setting, and plot in literacy discussions.

3. Providing opportunities for young readers to respond to texts through the use of digital media and fan cultures

My *Narnia*-related research reveals that new media spaces and practices have become central to the production and reception of books aimed at preadolescent readers. For many participants, the official website of a book, film, or franchise provides only one entry among many into a number of online forums, including fan-generated websites, child-produced spoof videos, photo-collages, and fan fiction posted online in private and public forums. These digital productions and spaces exemplify how new media provide opportunities for active engagement with older media. Moreover, many of these franchises involve online fan communities around the celebrity lives of actors, writers, and producers. These fan communities of tween readers may illustrate an allegiance to a character in a book that may not have been cultivated in response to the written text in isolation. This may be observed in fan sites dedicated to Emma Watson who plays Hermione in the Harry Potter films (2001–2008) and Georgie Henley, who plays Lucy in *The Chronicles of Narnia* film (2005).

A popular fan culture activity is the creation of montage music videos that edit and remix clips from favourite films or still images of specific characters and actors. A number of fan videos that may be found on YouTube (and other fan venues) integrate elements of Narnia with other textual narratives, characters, and franchises through the remixing of film clips, often with a soundtrack and sometimes subtitled dialogue. Often these videos illustrate alternative narratives created by young digital producers. For example, one fan video remixes scenes of Lucy throughout the Narnia film to "Breakaway" by Kelly Clarkson, the musical theme that sets the coming-of-age tone of the tween film *Princess Diaries 2* (2004). This remixing results in an emphasis on *The Lion, the Witch, and the Wardrobe* as a transformative narrative for Lucy. The montage of selected clips of Lucy at different scenes throughout the film reflects a similar visual style as the music video. Rather than a chronological progression, the editing of images seems to be matched with the speed of the music and the meaning of the lyrics.

Designing fan websites for a book/film franchise

Building on these examples from fan culture, particularly fan videos and fan sites, there are a number of digital activities that can be adapted for classroom work for individuals and groups. David Buckingham in *Media Education: Literacy, learning and contemporary culture* (2003) proposes that "we need to understand the role of the media as a dynamic and multi-faceted process, a matter of the interaction between *technologies*, *economies*, *texts*, and *audiences*" (18). Following Buckingham's consideration of this argument in media education, I wish to apply this frame to be used as a guide for lessons about website design and production.

A series of lessons dedicated to the production and design of fan websites might be implemented as follows:

a. Divide class into groups of 3 to 5 students who will make up the website design team.
b. Each group may be given a different website design assignment. Each group may be assigned a website related to the same book/media franchise such as Narnia. For example, one group is a fan site, one is a commercial site for Disney, one group is an educational site for teachers, and so on. Alternatively, each group could be assigned a different franchise and might decide among themselves what type of site they will design.
c. These group discussions could result in team proposals for their websites that they might present to the class or complete in written form. Depending on technical resources available, these discussions might evolve into media production activities, including website construction and digital video editing using classroom or computer lab resources.

Key Discussion Topics for Website Design Group Project

Discussion 1		
Preliminary discussion about the website to be designed	• What is the purpose of the website? • What type of website is this?	• Is this a fan site? • A commercial site to sell products? • A promotional site for a new series?
Discussion 2		
Economies of production (Industry)	• How does your site connect to other websites? • Other products of the same brand? • Other companies, advertisers?	• Who has access to this website? • Who is allowed to use information on the site? • What will be censored?
Discussion 3		
Audiences	• Who is your target audience (age, gender, nationality, special interests, fans?) • How will you appeal to them? • Will you test the site on potential users?	• How will users of the site find out about it? • Will users of the site be able to participate in chats, comments, add their own material?
Discussion 4		
Technology/web design choices	• What modes and features will be used on the site (audio, interactive video, pop-up windows etc.) ? • What font, colour, size of images? • What will be central image on the site? • What special features would the site have?	• Categories for analysis and discussion questions from Chart 1 may be used here as well.

Figure 11.3.

Taking it further: Cross-media literacies and children's book franchises

In order to engage readers who experience texts outside of the classroom as multimedia phenomena, it is crucial that teachers provide opportunities for students to share their extracurricular media knowledge, skills, and experiences in school settings. Students in your classrooms may already be active online participants as visitors, members or producers of fan sites or fan video forums related to a range of texts. Many of these creative and critical activities with digital media may be integrated or drawn upon as central or supplementary literacy activities. These cross-media Narnia texts and activities should be viewed as only a starting point for teachers looking for innovative ways to integrate media and popular culture texts with teaching around children's literature and literacy. In the quickly changing digital environment, our students often have access to the most valuable resources to enrich the literacy curriculum.

REFERENCES

Buckingham, David. 2003. *Media education: Literacy, learning and contemporary culture.* Cambridge: Polity Press.

High School Musical. 2006. Dir. Kenny Ortega. With Zac Efron, Vanessa Anne Hudgens, Ashley Tisdale. First Street Films, Salty Pictures, Walt Disney Pictures.

Livingstone, S. 2002. *Young people and new media: Childhood and the changing media environment.* London: Sage Publications.

Mackey, Margaret. 2002. *Literacies across media: Playing the text.* London: RoutledgeFalmer.

The Princess Diaries 2: Royal Engagement. 2004. Dir. Garry Marshall. With Anne Hathaway, Julie Andrews. BrownHouse Productions: Walt Disney Pictures.

Worldwide grosses. 2009. *The Chronicles of Narnia Box Office Mojo.* <http://www.boxofficemojo.com/movies/?id=narnia.htm> (accessed March 21, 2009).

RESOURCES

Books and websites

C.S. Lewis Pte, Ltd., Disney Enterprises Inc. and Walden Media. 2005. *Lucy's adventure: The quest for Aslan, the Great Lion.* London: HarperCollins Publishers Ltd.

Lewis, C.S. 1950/2005. *The lion, the witch and the wardrobe.* New York: HarperCollins,.

The chronicles of Narnia: The lion, the witch, and the wardrobe. Dir. Andrew Adamson. With Georgie Henley, Skandar Keynes, William Moseley, Anna Popplewell, Tilda Swinton, James McAvoy. Disney Pictures, Walden Media, Lamp-Post Productions. [DVD release: 2006.]

The chronicles of Narnia: The lion, the witch, and the wardrobe. 2005. Dir. Marilyn Fox. With Richard Dempsey, Sophie Cooke, Jonathan R. Scott, Sophie Wilcox, Barbara Kellerman. British Broadcasting Corporation (BBC), TVC London, WonderWorks. Original release date: November 13, 1988 (UK). [Collector's edition DVD release: 2005]

The lion, the witch and the wardrobe. Dir. Bill Melendez. Bill Melendez Productions, Children's Television Workshop, Episcopal Radio-TV Foundation, Pegbar Productions, TV Cartoons. Original release date: April 1, 1979 (US/UK).

Narnia website links (accessed March 30, 2009)

C.S. Lewis Institute: Discipleship of heart and mind: <http://www.cslewisinstitute.org/cslewis/index.htm>.

Walt Disney Studios Home Entertainment: <http://adisney.go.com/disneypictures/narnia/index.html>.

Harper Collins Children's Books: <http://books.narnia.com/>.

Narnia Fans website: <http://www.narniafans.com/>

<http://www.narniaweb.com/>

<http://www.thelionscall.com/>

Other Narnia references

Brodie, Ian. 2005. *Cameras in Narnia: How the lion, the witch and the wardrobe came to life*. HarperCollins.

Ford, Paul. 2005. *Companion to Narnia, Revised Edition*. HarperSanFrancisco.

Jacobs, Alan. 2005. *The Narnian: The life and imagination of C.S. Lewis*. HarperSanFrancisco.

Moore, Perry. 2005. *The chronicles of Narnia–The lion, the witch and the wardrobe: Official illustrated movie companion*. Disney Enterprises Inc. and HarperCollins.

Wagner, Richard. 2005. *C.S. Lewis & Narnia for dummies*. For Dummies.

A guide for using The lion, the witch and the wardrobe in the classroom. 2000. Teacher Created Resources.

The lion, witch & wardrobe Study Guide. 1993. Progeny Press.

Further reading

A number of international literacy education researchers have been studying the role of media, multimodality, and popular culture in recreational and classroom settings. The list of references below highlights some relevant titles if you are interested in reading more about ways to analyze, discuss, and use cross-media and popular culture texts in literacy education contexts.

Burn, A. and D. Parker. 2003. *Analysing media texts*. Continuum Research Methods Series. Ed. Richard Andrews. London: Continuum.

Cope, B. and M. Kalantzis, eds. 2000. *Multiliteracies: Literacy learning and the design of social futures*. London: Routledge.

Dyson, A. H. 2003. *The brothers and sisters learn to write: Popular literacies in childhood and school cultures*. New York: Teacher's College Press.

Kress, G. and T. van Leeuwen. 2001. *Multimodal discourse: The modes and media of contemporary communication*. London: Oxford University Press.

Marsh, J. and E. Millard. 2000. *Literacy and popular culture: Using children's culture in the classroom*. London: Paul Chapman.

Pahl, K. and J. Rowsell. 2005. *The new literacy studies in the classroom*. London: Paul Chapman.

Chapter 12

Toytexts: Critically Reading Children's Playthings

Linda Cameron and Kimberly Bezaire

Kids today are plugged in, programmed, primed by the media, plagued with digital technologies, marketed to, and engaged in screen time by the hour. Pushing buttons to optimum effect, they expect life to happen effectively, perfectly, and with immediacy. Changes to leisure and lifestyle have profoundly affected children's "conditions of learning"—their play-learning lives at home, school, and within their communities. Is this good? Are there concerns? Are technologies or toys welcome at school? Will they support literacy and learning both at home and at school? Do technologies interfere with learning or do they enhance it? What are the roles of toys as texts in this dilemma? What is the power and potential of play today?

In considering the impact of digital technologies and "hurried" childhood agendas within the context of new literacies and multiliteracies theories, we recognize and define consumer cross-marketing as multimodal digital technology, and children's playthings as "toytexts"—objects that involve children in social meaning-making processes through their acquisition, interaction, and play. *Toytexts are symbolic objects, material artifacts which convey meaning and references to the social world, as children decode and invest meaning in these objects and in play contexts.*

Within today's age of consumer marketing, toytexts are pedagogically and personally powerful. The broader range and number of products marketed directly to children are more numerous than ever before. Advertising messages of all sorts are targeted directly to the child. Add the powerful word-of-mouth bragging of the children to each other about what they have and what it can do, and the kids are hooked. The most popular and pervasive of these toytexts are intertextually linked to a burgeoning array of other products — television shows, DVDs, CD-ROMs, websites, dolls, games, clothing, food, and cosmetic products creating a web of interrelated texts to capture the kids. As children's imaginations, interest, media links, and "purchasing power" are ensnared in this ever-widening and complex web of products and promotions, we recognize the tension in this web, and invite you to question with us. Do children need to be protected from them or might we invite or allow these texts into our homes and classrooms? Although we might ignore their pervasiveness, they are already there in children's minds, memories, stories, and interests. Even if we do relegate the toys to outside the classroom, they sneak in stealthily — so maybe we should acknowledge these toytexts and use them with care. Maybe these toytexts need educating?

Role of play in literacy learning

As teachers, parents, and administrators, we can be assured that play holds significant language and literacy learning potential — the evidence is clear (Podlozny 2000; Roskos and Christie 2001). When fully engaged in the artistry of play, children display creativity, voice, improvisation, composition, experimentation, exploration, personal expression, choice, and ownership — some of the most sophisticated high-order literacy skills! Children's inner speech and ideas become visible with participants "consciously choosing symbols and modes of representation that help them organize and articulate their inner thoughts" (Cameron and Bezaire 2007; Kendrick 2005, 9). Story comprehension, reading achievement, reading readiness, and writing are all shown to benefit from inclusion of drama in the classroom, particularly structured enactment when the classroom leader engages in and models role play (Podlozny 2000). Challenging a back-to-basics skill and drill approach, play and drama experiences are not extras to be used as enrichment and reward for our highest achievers but rather are "engagers." Significantly, the positive effects of drama instruction have been shown to be greater for children from lower socioeconomic status and for remedial readers (Podlozny 2000, 254). Play and drama offer powerful tools for teaching and learning, particularly within some of our more challenging teaching contexts. Toytexts and technology have a role here.

Despite this evidence, play is held hostage by unrealistic standards of academic excellence and hurried childhoods (Cameron 2006; Elkind 1994). Leading experts in education and pediatric health are sounding the warning — for many complex reasons. Today's children largely lack the playtime, spaces, and freedom that their parents and grandparents enjoyed (Alliance for Childhood 2004; American Academy of Pediatrics 2007). As a teacher, you are likely aware of the signs and symptoms — epidemic child obesity, increasing hours in front of TV and computer screens, overprotected kids with overscheduled lives, others who are living in need — few living in neighbourhoods where children feel free to roam and play. From our dialogue and work with teachers, pre-service students, and parents, we hear a chorus of voices, mourning the loss of childhood play and of childhood itself. As we consider the challenges of ensuring essential play opportunities for today's children, new literacies perspectives may allow us to look at child's play and play in school from a fresh, dynamic 21st-century perspective. What is the role of toytexts and technologies in our classrooms?

Texts as toys: A genre of children's literature

Theo Heras, Children's Literature Resource Collection Specialist at The Lillian H. Smith Osborne Collection Library, offers an expert perspective on the world of children's literature, both past and present. From the Little Golden Books of the 1930s, first published featuring Walt Disney's Mickey Mouse, to Richard Scarry's Busytown Books series, to today's microchip-embedded books featuring a myriad of sound effects and popular media characters, "there are," muses Heras, "those books which you're more likely to find in the toy box than on the bookshelf." In today's era of cross-marketing and digital technologies, the books in this toytext genre are increasing and becoming more and more enhanced.

In the expanding children's book market, publishers have steadily focused on visual appeal, and have found that hands-on features both charm and engage young readers. Traditional features such as pop-ups and revolving pictures have been revolutionized, as exemplified by children's book creators Robert Sabuda (*Encyclopedia Prehistorica Dinosaurs: The Definitive Pop-Up*) and David A. Carter (*600 Black Spots: A Pop-up for Children of All Ages*). Allan Ahlberg's *The Jolly Postman*, which includes envelopes and removable letters written from the perspective of various fairytale characters, continues to be a very popular example of toytext books. These include features such as flaps, cutaways, removable notes, and play objects. Books such as *Dragonology* and its companion series feature high-interest topics, an encyclopedic-style, and a range of visual and tactile texts. The books themselves are play objects. Their emphasis on how-to text offers invitations to make-believe and pretend—to act as text-user and participant, deepening the possibility of engagement and comprehension (Luke and Freebody 1999). This genre and style of picture book can be considered toy as much as text—a toytext!

Similarly, consider what other books may be included in the toytext genre—what are their defining characteristics? Texts that are fun and engaging, have visual appeal, and invite active participation and make-believe. Wallace Edwards' *The Painted Circus* draws the reader into active engagement with the artist's optical illusion and visual puzzles. Graeme Base's books *Animalia, The Water Hole,* and *The Discovery of Dragons: New Research Revealed* prompt readers to probe the sophisticated, complicated artistically rich illustrations to solve problems and mysteries, often resulting in repeated, shared reading. Bob McLeod's *Superhero ABC* offers comic-book-style illustration on over-sized pages and engaging characters who invite active imagination and superhero play. On a recent series of home visits with young emergent and beginning readers, we were given personal tours of children's playrooms, toy boxes, and bookshelves. In addition to the *Ology* series and pop-up books, children's favourites included the *Where's Waldo?* and *I Spy* series and, most often, books that are linked to popular media such as movies, TV shows, sports teams, animé characters, and toy products. Whatever the latest trend—in these instances *Scoobie-Doo*, *Star Wars*, *Hannah Montana*, and *High School Musical*—these are the first choice of so many children, not just the reluctant readers for whom these books offer fun entry points for literacy experience. While these books disrupt traditional notions of narrative and story ("good literature"), we argue that they offer opportunities to participate in literacy in the broadest sense of the word—these texts offer invitations to pretend and create, to make believe.

What sort of books prompt play, lending themselves to inspire make-believe and drama? How can highly commercial books and toys—items that teachers and librarians have traditionally seen as suspect, frivolous or of low quality—contribute to children's literacies, both at school and beyond? Rather than relegating these high-interest objects to cubbies and backpacks or pushing play and popular play objects to the margins of our classrooms, let's consider the multimodal ways in which children use them and how they are intertextually linked to other texts, particularly in digital technologies.

Indiana Jones and a toy snake in grade one!

Ethan (all names are pseudonyms) arrived at school, proudly showing off his arms to a group of his classmates—they are covered with temporary tattoos featuring ferocious snakes with curving bodies and sharp teeth. At group time, the noise level rises as the children boisterously admire the tattoos. "Snakes! Why'd it have to be snakes?" exclaimed Ethan and a group of his classmates erupt into laughter, and the classroom teacher recognizes a recurrent popular theme. Ethan was referencing Indiana Jones, a movie character currently featured in an array of products and movie promotions. With connections to a new summer blockbuster, toys, Lego, videogames and fast-food promotion, knowledge and ownership of all things Indiana have been powerful status symbols within the classroom. Although this aversion to snakes is well known among the boys, as the Indiana character's one fear (the chink in his macho persona), a group of boys seem fascinated rather than repulsed by the reptiles.

Later, at the art table, the teacher is compelled to stop a trio of boys using felt-tip markers to decorate their own arms with snake tattoos; instead she offers them sheets of thin vellum, and they are soon taping handmade images to each other's arms and legs. Ethan joins in, crafting the shape of an

'S' which he tapes to his chest and declares, "I'm Snakeman!" Having noted this emerging interest, and somewhat relieved that the boys have stopped fashioning whips (another Indiana Jones reference!) from the art materials, the teacher locates several rubber and wooden toy snakes and places them in places of interest throughout the classroom ... a young boy roars across the classroom dramatically sobbing, "I got a snakebite and I am going to die!". A popular wooden toy snake was in the classroom science centre where he had been digging wrigglers in a bushel of dirt. The children urged him into the "hospital" to get fixed up, and the discussion began earnestly with the "doctor"(quickly appointed and dressed in the lab coat) about whether or not the snake was poisonous. The classroom teacher overheard and entered the play as a poison expert surgeon, directing the boys to a book about snakes so that they could identify the villain. The "treatment" needed to be appropriate to the particular snake. While "treating" the bite, she invited others into the drama to take over his recovery care.

From there, the questions about how to treat snake bites, where certain snakes live, and what can happen to you if you get bites, and on and on ... led the boys with several other students into some very intriguing research.

The snake inquiry caught on and soon almost everyone was reading about snakes (looking at pictures and accessing what they could), writing and drawing, and definitely talking about snakes. Everyone was developing expertise in ophiology, the study of snakes. "Did you know that snake in Greek is *ophis*?" exclaimed Tony.

The teacher knew little about snakes except that she was afraid of them but, then, so was Indiana Jones! Conversations on the topics of fear and courage emerged: Does it make sense to be afraid of snakes? Why do people have fears, and what are strategies for overcoming them? Gender issues were discussed, as children and teacher (then parents, relating home conversations) interrogated stereotypes about fears, courage, and what it might mean to be brave as a boy, a girl, a human being, or a snake! Though Indiana's movie theme song became the class anthem for moments of bravery, he eventually did not dominate in moments of valour, bravery, and action.

The growing posters of language on charts included such concepts as venomous, venoms, and other poisons, antidotes, rectilinear locomotion, concertina climbing, and side winding. "Did you know that snakes have no eyelids?" a little boy asked. "What are eyelids for anyway?"... the inquiry went in another direction now. Another link to another concept. "How do our eyelids work?" The classroom mirror became an important pedagogical tool as the children crowded around examining their eyelids, lashes, eyebrows, and then experimented with facial expressions ... oh the language!

"Boy snakes love to fight!" With that statement, several boys who had wandered off came bounding back into the investigation. So much to learn! Geography and science—where and why do snakes live in certain places? How do they survive?

What kinds of snakes are local? How are they related to lizards and other reptiles? What is a reptile? Ecosystem!? What's that? Who are snake enemies, and what role do humans play in their peril and protection? How else, besides destroying, could Indiana get around them during his archaeological adventures? What advice would we give him? During these discussions, students came to discuss Indiana as a fictional character, relating his persona to those from other stories. "Heroes all have a weakness. Like Superman. His is kryptonite. That's poisonous to him." Admittedly, Indiana Jones maintained his appeal with the children, but his mass-marketed grip seemed to lessen somewhat as the children recognize him within the context of multiple texts.

Meanwhile, with all this talk of poison and danger, a group of girls started thinking about fairy tales and witches and spells, and they took the ideas to other worlds. The whole class began an inquiry about poisons in the classroom and at home and made charts and warning signs that incorporated icons marking dangerous substances. Huge signs marking DANGER, beware, warning, flashing in psychedelic paint choices were created and posted about the room. Literacy!

What did this project look like? It worked like a gigantic and developing website. It had charts with the ongoing developing questions recorded to follow, expository books about snakes, reptiles and poison to use for research, an increasing collection of folk and fairy tales that had a poison motif, empty containers that had the poison symbol on them, information from the government on poison control, stories written by the children involving poison and snakes and other gruesome things, and so on. There were lists of poisons to avoid—chemicals, plants, and animals. There were virtual visits to the Toronto Zoo and Natural History Museums, searching for facts and photographs, emailing experts with specific questions. There was talk, lots of talk. There was laughter and engagement. Stories. Feelings. Work, hard work! Thinking, questioning, a truly wonder-filled curriculum!

> "If the invitation is presented through available materials, space, time, story, inspiring ideas, questions, supportive scaffolding of caring adults, modelling and demonstrations, celebration of approximations and opportunities for fun, wonder-full learning will result.... That is, if (and only if) the conditions for their artistry allow for creativity, voice, improvisation, experimentation, exploration, developmental differences, personal expression, choice and ownership" (Cameron and Bezaire 2007, 127).

What did the teacher and the children learn? This is quite immeasurable, but evident—the project affected attitudes, behaviours, raised awareness, taught about how to do research, increased the amount of reading and writing for real purposes, informed the students about where to find resources and so on. What happened in that classroom far exceeded the teacher's expectations about the learning possibilities or the probabilities for these young children. This learning was not guided by a lesson plan or a commercially produced guide but rather came from the children who got the seeds of their ideas and inquiry from the current media and some toytexts and some very important make-believe!

The project culminated (actually it really never did end because the connections and reflections kept popping up with new links emerging) with a visit to the zoo and a visit from a man who brought several snakes for the children to visit with. The teacher even held the boa constrictor, her phobia under control!

Toys as text: Text as toys

What role do toys, technologies, playthings, and props have in these worthwhile activities, and how do they connect to our understandings of new literacies? How can texts be toyed with to invite deeper understanding, wonderment, and critical literacy opportunities? Contemporary childhood, characterized by high levels of consumer culture and electronic media, involves children in increasingly complex meaning making, characterized by literacies which are multimodal and intertextual. Popular children's toys offer an illustrative example, crossing a range of modes, messages, markets, and meanings. Though we may try to stop these consumer texts at the schoolroom door (how many of us would allow Bratz dolls, Game Boy games, or Star Wars light sabres to be physically played with in our classrooms?), their stories, themes, and suggestions... should we? Stephen Kline (1999), when considering the communicative power of toys, cautions that "in adopting this 'hands-off' attitude, (adults) are missing an important opportunity to communicate with children" regarding our own moral values and perspectives.

Toys do not simply represent child's play but are symbolic objects, "distinct cultural and material artefacts" communicating prevalent ideas about gender, childhood. and mass consumption (Kline 1999; Carrington 2003, 92). As a text, a toy has powerful pedagogic potential, intertextually connected through cross-marketing to a wide range of other media such as advertising, television programming, clothing lines, computer games, and fast food restaurants (Carrington 2003). "One of the key pedagogic features of consumer texts made for children is that they are rarely stand-alone. This is what makes them so pedagogically powerful" (Carrington 2003, 93). These texts risk going critically unexamined by child consumers, and adults alike. In comparison to the hurried and sophisticated child consumer, teachers and parents are often not as knowledgeable or informed in respect to the modes and messages embedded in children's consumer products (Carrington 2004).

Bratz dolls in grade 2

Three girls huddled whispering with a young woman dressed in less-than-conservative clothing—minimal skirt, bare midriff, high-heeled boots going up her long and lanky legs and over the knees, her face caked with an over-abundance of makeup, animé eyes oversized and seductive, carrying a backpack decorated with skull and crossbones. The girls' secretive tones kept the teacher on edge as she stepped closer to hear the conversation. With this Bratz doll, the seven-year-olds were talking about going shopping for a new "sassy" outfit which promises to make them feel better. Arguments about the shopping plans and the resultant "date" heightened the volume of their discourse because one of the girls wanted to align the script to one she had seen on the Bratz television show, website, and DVDs.

Was there only one way to have things happen already scripted by the media? What invitations for composing and enacting story do toys present? Chloe, the doll, has an obvious genre. She is teenaged, sexy, she comes with an array of accessories that add to the probable narrative, she is brash and seductive... is she "the sort of girl" who would be gentle, nurturing, and ready to play school? Is she someone who you would even want these girls to have as a babysitter? How do these little girls know the discourse frame that is appropriate for Chloe? How do they know how to relate to her and with her world? What will the story be that they develop? What is Chloe's text? What are the stories developing in the heads of the girls playing with her? While adults may assume that today's popular dolls are simply reminiscent of yesterday's "fashion doll" or dress-up play, Chloe is a text whose messages—about gender, consumption—are intertextually linked to advertisement, multimedia and popular media.

Is there room in your classroom for dolls? Where might Chloe fit the grade 2 curriculum? Imagine harnessing the engagement of these young girls in a variety of possibilities. They might write a play script, compose a story about her future, design some clothes or furniture for her, write a diary in Chloe's voice, become engaged with you, the teacher, in a role as a vocational counsellor doing some critical work in role, pushing Chloe and her friends to consider how they might find direction in their lives, conversing about health issues, issues of privilege and culture... the list goes on. Banning such toytexts as Bratz dolls removes many possibilities for discussing and working through many critical issues. If Chloe had not come into the classroom, there would not have been any real, meaningful, and relevant context through which to contemplate some very serious issues with these young but too grown-up girls.

Bratz marketers claim that they are "the only girls with a passion for fashion." We were able to contemplate together if that is a valid claim and, if so, would we like to be defined that way? Doing some media literacy inquiry by critically exploring the Bratz website together, we see what the marketers are encouraging, and then question what that means to the girls. The talking Bratz dolls were very disturbing to our young market investigators. Chloe provided a powerful provocation to read, write, talk, think, question, negotiate, create, and, hopefully, to reflect on what really matters to each one of the girls as they gained experience in working through some pretty important issues critically.

The boys in the class were fascinated with the discussion and presentation of the findings that the girls made about the products that were targeted at them and wondered where the marketers were "sucking them in." A heated discussion ensued and the teacher suggested a list be made, and the research began.

Open-ended toytexts

While we recognize the importance of playfully and critically engaging with and alongside children in their explorations of popular commercial toytexts,

> "we need to provide a myriad of invitations in richly resourced and inviting settings that suggest wonderful ideas to children. We need to keep in mind that different experiences, stories, props, spawn varied invitations and questions to different children. We need to accept each child's ideas and creativity and value his or her queries and investigations as they wonder, play, and learn. We need to provide safe and caring environments so that children can have the confidence to try out their wonderful ideas, believing that they have the support and trust of their teachers" (Cameron & Bezaire 2007, 133).

Open-ended playthings—blocks, sand and water, figurines, stuffed animals—are also toytexts that invite storying and make-believe, with children sometimes linking this play, too, to digital technology and current themes in popular culture, sometimes allowing children to transcend limited commercial scripts and play with deeper meaning and understanding.

Dinosaurs in the sandbox

In a grade one classroom, the children were playing with dinosaurs in the sandbox, their own Jurassic Park. These dinosaur toytexts had different meanings to the individuals playing with them because of the children's prior experiences and knowledge about them. The children decided that they could interview their dinosaurs to find out what life had been like for them, and immediately the class palaeontology experts became the Rex of choice. They were taking turns in role as various dinosaurs, and inventing imaginary answers while dramatizing their stories in the sandbox filled with rocks, artificial trees, and bits of branches. One of the children suggested that they could pick some of the best questions to explore and find out more expert answers from books and the web by asking older children (their reading buddies) to help them. The teacher was ready with clipboard and pen to record their inquiries. Out came the books from the library, up came the topic on the computer, and the children pored over the resources with sandy toys in hand. "Which one is that?" "What does he eat?" "Are there girl dinosaurs.... there has to be mommies?" "Do babies come in eggs?" "Which one is the strongest?" and "Are some dinosaurs still alive ... are alligators dinosaur cousins?" Toytexts provided the engagement and the invitations, spawning all sorts of literacies.

After some time to play dinosaurs, to research dinosaurs, to visit them online at the museum, the young palaeontologists made up puppet plays, called a day in the life of... and produced them for the kindergarten class. All this began and flourished because of the toytexts—and of course the insatiable fascination of children with palaeontology!

Have we lost sight of what really matters in this time of standardized, tested curriculum? Have we forgotten that our learning curve escalates when we are permitted to chase our own robust questions? Have we lost faith in the curiosity of children? Have we forgotten how much we learn through play?

Let's imagine a classroom that would have opportunities for play as a fundamental part of the literacy curriculum, a curriculum that invites and celebrates and inspires the development of multiple literacies. Think about the conversations about life and literature, about the students' interests and yours and how they can be playful.

"What about guns?" teachers ask. Aggression and action, embodied in superheroes and war toys, are prevalent aspects of boys' play, popular culture, and imaginative lives from superhero play in Junior Kindergarten through video game playing in middle school years (and, indeed, adulthood!) This is a tough call. What could we learn if we allowed these toytexts into our classrooms?

If grade 5s were in charge

Most of the grade 5 boys have largely set aside toy box treasures in favour of popular Wii and Xbox video games. Though this virtual play happens outside of school, these worlds of action, aggression, and power struggle surface during less structured social time and open writing times within the classroom. In November, actual Lego blocks and toy soldiers once again replace their virtual counterparts when the class designs battlefield dioramas in their exploration and explanation of Remembrance Day and other civic ceremonies. Some of the children's robust questions included—Who decides to go to war and who decides when it will stop? Who is "in charge"?

We listened in while the teacher began a lesson on government structure and then paused to ask what the kids might consider doing if they were in charge of the country, inspired by *If I was in charge of the world* by Judith Viorst. He invited students to work with a partner and take clipboards to jot notes to track their thinking as they talked and played with the possibilities of power, real power, if they had it. He had put some prompts up to challenge their thinking and moved about the room listening, laughing, questioning, supporting, cajoling, "playing" with the students, sometimes in role as an advocate, sometimes a lobbyist, sometimes a visiting dignitary, and sometimes as the teacher. What would they do? How would they live? What might their priorities be? Who would their friends and enemies be? What political structures might work best? Then the pairs were blended to share ideas, to prioritize the expressed needs of the country, to propose solutions, and to come up with a government structure that they believed might work and why.

After this initial playful session, the students were invited to keep thinking about the questions that had emerged, to do some research, to keep the questions alive. Ideas and issues were shared with the whole class. Some big issues were posted on the charts, more time for developing more ideas was promised, and they were challenged to keep designing and editing their ideas. After several days and lots of talk and drafting of thoughts and the development of questions, they came up with several ideas about who they might like to interview about their questions, who they might lobby, what they might like to write to their local parliamentarian. One group of students volunteered to research and report on how their federal government worked; another was challenged to look at more local structures. The classroom buzzed with energy, and conversations continued during the breaks. Another list was growing on the bulletin board about political and social issues and concerns the students had that were relevant to them in particular. One student wondered aloud what it would take to get elected, and that led to questions about student government and how they could take on some responsibility in their local system. Play! Make believe! From video games, movies, action figures to deep contemplation about reality and important issues.

Kids today are still full of wonder that has been fuelled by their exposure to the world—to a degree far beyond our own childhood comprehension. They can see the world through the screen. Knowledge is no longer bound in a row of encyclopaedia volumes—with the click of the mouse, they have easy access to answers from world experts who can stimulate more learning. Thankfully, we teachers no longer need to know everything, just how to help our students get to the resources they need. We do need to listen for our student's robust questions, however, to facilitate their inquiry. We need to keep up-to-date with what influences their thinking and is current culturally in their world. We need to know our kids and trust their questions.

Should we fear inviting toytexts into our classrooms? If they are not morally or physically threatening... why not invite them in? Just think about how they might inspire the children's thinking as their books, their literature do. Toys are texts and texts are toys. Let's play! LEGO.

REFERENCES

Alliance for Childhood. 2004. Childhood essentials: Fostering the full range of human capacities (chapter 3 in *Fool's Gold; A Critical Look at Computers in Childhood*, Colleen Cordes and Edward Miller, eds. <http://www.allianceforchildhood.org/fools_gold> (accessed March 31, 2009).

American Academy of Pediatrics. 2007. The importance of play in promoting healthy child development and maintaining strong parent-child bonds. *Pediatrics, 119*(1), 2007. Available at <http://www.aap.org/pressroom/playFINAL.pdf> (accessed March 31, 2009).

Cameron, Linda. 2006. Play held hostage by the "bully"—excellence. Keynote presentation at the Learning through the Arts Conference, Toronto, Canada. Available in *Touchstone,* Conference Issue: Fall 2006 at: <http://www.oise.utoronto.ca/newsletters/december_06/> (accessed March 31, 2009).

Cameron, Linda and Kimberly Bezaire. 2007. Art-full play: Wonder-full learning. In M. Hachiya (ed.), *Prospects for new early childhood education through art*. Yamagata, Japan: Research Center for Children's Art Education, Tohoku University of Art and Design.

Carrington, Victoria. 2003. "I'm in a bad mood. Let's go shopping": Interactive dolls, consumer culture and a 'glocalized' model of literacy. *Journal of Early Childhood Literacy*, 3 (1), 83–98.

Carrington, Victoria. 2004. Texts and literacies of the Shi Jinrui. *British Journal of Sociology of Education*, 25 (2), 215–228.

Elkind, David. 1994. *Ties that stress: The new family imbalance*. Cambridge, MA: Harvard University Press.

Luke, Alan and Peter Freebody. 1999. A map of possible practices: Further notes on the four resources model. *Practically Primary*, 4 (2), 5–8.

Kendrick, Maureen. 2005. Playing house: A "sideways" glance at literacy and identity in early childhood. *Journal of Early Childhood Literacy*, 5 (1), 5–28.

Kline, Stephen. 1999. *Toys as media: The role of toy design, promotional TV and mother's reinforcement in the young males (3-6). Acquisition of pro-social play scripts for rescue hero action toys*. ITRA Conference. 18 June, 1999, Halmstadt, Sweden. Available at: <http://www2.sfu.ca/media-lab/research/toys/toymedia.pdf> (accessed March 31, 2009).

Podlozny, Ann. 2000. Strengthening verbal skills through the use of classroom drama: A clear link. *Journal of Aesthetic Education*, 34 (3-4), 239–275.

Roskos, Kathleen and James Christie. 2001. Examining the play-literacy interface: A critical review and future directions. *Journal of Early Childhood Literacy*, 1 (1), 59–89.

RESOURCES

Children's books

Ahlberg, Allan. 2006. *The jolly postman*. New York: Hachette Book Group/ LB Kids.

Base, Graeme. 1987. *Animalia*. New York: Abrams Books for Young Readers.

——————. 1996. *The discovery of dragons: New research revealed*. New York: Abrams Books for Young Readers.

——————. 2001. *The water hole*. New York: Abrams Books for Young Readers.

Carter, David A.. 2006. *Blue 2: A pop-up for children of all ages*. New York: Little Simon.

——————. 2007. *600 black spots: A pop-up for children of all ages*. New York: Little Simon.

Drake, Ernest. 2003. *Dragonology: The complete book of dragons*. Somerville, Mass: Candlewick Press.

Edwards, Wallace. 2006. *The extinct files: My science project.* Toronto: Kids Can Press.

_____. 2007. *The painted circus.* Toronto: Kids Can Press.

Marcus, Leonard S. 2007. *Golden legacy: How Golden Books won children's hearts, changed publishing forever, and became an American icon along the way.* New York: Random House.

McLeod, Bob. 2006. *Superhero ABC.* New York: HarperCollins.

Sabuda, Robert and Matthew Reinhart. 2005. *Encyclopedia prehistorica. Dinosaurs.* Cambridge MA: Candlewick Press.

_____. 2007. *Encyclopedia prehistorica. Mega-beasts.* Cambridge MA: Candlewick Press.

Viorst, Judith. 1981. *If I were in charge of the world and other worries: Poems for children and their parents.* New York: Atheneum.

Websites (accessed March 31, 2009)

Ology series: http://www.ologyworld.com/ Candlewick Press Inc.

Canadian Encyclopedia/Dinosaur Hunting in Western Canada: <http://www.thecanadianencyclopedia.com/index.cfm?PgNm=TCE&Params=A1ARTA0002297>

DinosaurNews: <http://www.dinosaurnews.org/>.

Dinosaur Provincial Park—UNESCO World Heritage Site:<http://whc.unesco.org/en/list/71>.

Drumheller, Alberta, Canada: <http://www.dinosaurvalley.com>.

Manitoba Museum: Why do we find dinosaurs in Alberta, Canada? <http://www.manitobamuseum.ca/mu_find.html>.

Natural History Museum/Dinosaurs and other extinct creatures: <http://www.nhm.ac.uk/nature-online/life/dinosaurs-other-extinct-creatures/index.html>.

Snakes (accessed March 31, 2009)

Canadian Encyclopedia Histor!ca: <http://www.thecanadianencyclopedia.com>

Manitoba Museum: <http:// www.manitobamuseum.ca>.

Nature Conservancy of Canada: <http://www.natureconservancy.ca>.

Nova Scotia Museum: <http://museum.gov.ns.ca/en/home/default.aspx>.

Snakes of North America: <http://www.pitt.edu/~mcs2/herp/SoNA.html>.

Toronto Zoo: <http://www.torontozoo.com>.

Section Five

Libraries: Literature and the Internet

Chapter 13

What Are All the Computers Doing in the Public Library?

Ken Setterington

For the past century, children in North America have been welcomed and encouraged to read through public library services. For example, in Canada during the year 2012 the Toronto Public Library will celebrate 100 years of children's services; the New York Public Library has already celebrated its centenary of children's services. Introducing children to books and encouraging reading has always been at the centre of the work that our libraries have done for children. However, it is important to today's user to acknowledge how technology has changed our services to children as libraries move into the second century of service.

The public library has long been thought of as the people's university. Access to information and the pursuit of lifelong learning have been trademarks for the public library. For those struggling with reading or unable to read in English, assistance in the form of classes and tutoring has had a rich tradition. Library services to children have concentrated on the enjoyment and learning that comes from reading and the encouragement of a thirst for knowledge. Children's librarians have long sought to introduce the right book to the right child at the right time. The knowledge that the right book in a child's hands—when they are most ready for it—may not only introduce a child to the delights that can be found through reading but also encourage an enduring love for reading. In addition to the presentation of fiction—traditionally the choice of reading material presented—librarians have also taught children the skills necessary to successfully locate the many resources found in the public library. In the past 100 years there have been many changes to the delivery of library services to children, but the basic philosophy has remained the same. Children deserve excellent library service and the best materials that can be offered to them.

In the early years of public library service, children were invited to attend storytimes, and parents were encouraged to read to their children; much of the children's librarians' time was spent finding the best books to introduce to children who were reading on their own. Libraries are now introducing children to the joy of reading at the earliest ages and are striving to encourage the joy of reading to young children through work with parents, caregivers, childcare workers, and basically anyone who interacts with preschool children. Libraries across Canada and the United States have adopted and adapted a program developed by the American Library Association—*Every Child Ready To Read*. The program is based on six literacy skills that need to be developed in children from birth to 5 years of age:

- Print Motivation
- Phonological Awareness
- Vocabulary
- Narrative Skills
- Print Awareness
- Letter Knowledge

These basic skills have now been incorporated into the preschool activities in many public libraries.

The Toronto Public Library has identified the six skills in simplified terms in the hope that newcomers and parents with difficulty reading would be able to grasp the concepts more easily, as follows:

- I like books—Print Motivation
- I hear words—Phonological Awareness
- I know words—Vocabulary
- I can tell a story—Narrative Skills
- I see words—Print Awareness
- I see letters—Letter Knowledge

The presentation and teaching of these skills has been incorporated into all programs that are conducted for preschool children and those working with them. One innovation in practice has been the use of the computer to enhance children's experiences with books. Libraries across North America have introduced specific preschool areas into their children's departments; they feature literacy activities that help children acquire the six literacy skills listed above.

At the opening of one such KidsStop recently, it was great fun to watch the young children rush into the area and discover the activities that had been developed for them. Their first destination was a rocket that can provide not only visual delight but also space for an impromptu puppet theatre. The rocket thus serves to encourage narrative skills. As enticing as the rocket ship was, the children rushed off to explore other activities. The huge board book mounted on the wall, the wall of turning blocks, the wooden puzzles mounted on a table, and the special light pen were all interesting, but the children spent the most time at the child-size computer with the track-ball mouse and ear phones.

The computer is loaded with stories from tumblebooks.com. Children can sit with an adult and read stories together on the computer. With earphones they can hear the story being read—sometimes by the author or an accomplished reader—and read the story along with the reader because the text is highlighted as the story is read aloud. It really is like having a talented reader present a favourite book to you. Computers designed specifically for preschool children are a common feature in libraries across North America.

During the past 100 years, children's books became brighter and more colourful, but the basic book format remained the same until the introduction of books onto computers. Despite the changed format, children greatly enjoy the opportunity to read books on a computer. More and more companies and libraries are finding ways to promote books and reading online. When visiting the website of any large public library system, one can quickly find a variety of books available online. On the website of The Screen Actors Guild Foundation, famous actors read favourite children's books (at Book Pals Storyline Online). This site provides a storytime experience which is almost as good as having someone read to you in person. Children can listen and watch Al Gore read William Steig's *Brave Irene* or Pamela Reed read *Stellaluna* by Janell Cannon. On the site, the text is written under the image of the reader so that a child can read along. Stories Online provides a very thoughtful and entertaining alternative to the ever-popular online games for children and their parents.

In addition to online books that are available to children in English, books in a variety of other languages can be found at the International Children's Digital Library (ICDL). The goal of the ICDL, as stated on the website, is "to build a collection ... that represents outstanding historical and contemporary books from throughout the world. Ultimately, the Foundation aspires to have every culture and language represented so that every child can know and appreciate the riches of children's literature from the world community." In its mission statement, the ICDL outlines its rationale: "As families move from Kenya to Finland or Brazil to Mexico or Viet Nam to California, books published in their native country or in their first language often must be left behind. In their new homelands, it may be difficult, if not impossible, to find children's books from their cultures and in their mother tongue. Parents have little access to the books and stories from their youth to pass on to the next generation. Many children must grow up without knowledge of their family's heritage and first language. A fundamental principle of the Foundation is that children and their families deserve to have access to the books of their culture, as well as the majority culture, regardless of where they live."

Through the children's digital library, young readers and their parents can find books in fifty different languages; for example, the traditional fairy tale, *The Story of the Three Little Pigs* illustrated by L. Leslie Brooks, is available to read in English, Chinese (traditional), French, Italian, Portuguese, Spanish, and Turkish. The book *The Blue Sky* by Adrea Petrlik Huseinovi is available in Croatian, English, Italian, and Spanish. Thus, the book collection of any public library is greatly enhanced by online literature, which offers material that would be difficult to purchase. Because parents are encouraged to read to their children in their mother tongue, reading materials are sought out for purchase in many different languages. However, they are not always easy to find; so the books available on the International Children's Digital Library are considered a great resource.

Library programs that involve reading and telling stories use technologies that allow children greater access to stories in a variety of formats. Audio books and kits with book and audiotape or CD have been very popular, but stories without a printed text are very useful in building narrative skills, vocabulary, and phonological awareness. Stories are available on the telephone throughout the United States and Canada for children in Putnam County, or San Francisco, or Toronto to listen to. These are popular services; for example, the Toronto Public Library's Dial-A-Story, which began in 1989, offers children of different age groups a range of stories to listen to over the phone. In 2007, over 300,000 calls were made to Dial-A-Story. Children first get to choose whether they will hear stories for younger or older children. The stories are available in 12 languages representing the most popular languages in the Toronto area, including English, French, Cantonese, Mandarin, Italian, Spanish, Polish, Portuguese, Somali, Tamil, Gujarati, and Urdu.

Children who visit TPL's KidsStop find a telephone with a direct line to Dial-A-Story. Many of these stories are also available on children's websites such as *KidsSpace* on *Hear-A-Story*, where they can listen to the stories online. Other sites that have amazing stories online are the Enoch Pratt Free Library in Baltimore, Maryland, which presents "e-stories" produced with the support of the Institute of Museum and Library Services. When connecting with e-stories, the viewer can watch master storytellers tell stories from a variety of cultures and traditions. These storytellers, who have won multiple awards, provide a rich experience for their audience. Included in the roster of storytellers is a very young Imani Adrea, only 8 years old, telling the story of *Pee Wee and the Big, Green Spider*. Imani comes from a family with a rich tradition of storytelling and is an inspiration for viewers of all ages.

Stories and books are available and easily accessible through the Internet once you become aware of them. Librarians and teachers face the challenge of simply keeping up with the technology and becoming aware of the useful sites available throughout the world that promote literacy skills for children and their families. They should ensure that children and their parents are aware of Dial-A-Story or the International Children's Digital Library and the e-stories offered through online resources.

Any discussion of technology involves a discussion of access. Not all children have computers or Internet connections at home. But public libraries provide access to computers throughout the world. Librarians can encourage children to use the computer and get to know how best to find information while using it. The book *Research Ate My Brain* followed by *Research Virtuoso* and published by Annick Press were written by library staff to show youth how best to use the resources on the Net as well as in libraries. Training children to find information and reading materials online has now become an important component of public librarianship.

Access to computers is crucial in our digital age. Aside from providing access to high speed computers in the library, the Toronto Public Library participates with various city departments in a program entitled *Kids@Computers*. Through this program, children in families living on social assistance are able to get a scholarship that enables them to learn about the use of the computer at the library and, upon graduation, receive a free computer and free Internet access for one year. Since 2001, over 7,000 computers have been distributed to families in Toronto through TPL. Computers clearly provide greater opportunities to increase literacy for the children lucky enough to be in the program. The success of the program has become obvious as the youth who had received computers as children return after graduating from the program to act as volunteers in the computer training program.

Programs that target literacy are common in public libraries. One tutor-based program matches children who are not reading up to grade level in grades 1 through 6 with volunteer tutors for hourly sessions on a weekly basis. Each year, over 2,000 children participate in the program to receive assistance in developing their reading skills. Volunteers in the program face the challenge of finding reading material for each child that will hold their interest, that they will want to read, either on their own or with assistance. The goal of finding the right book for the right child at the right time is crucial within this program.

Another program that directly targets non-readers, especially boys, is the newly designed program, *Literacy through HipHop*. In this program, children in grades 5 through 8 who are not reading are invited to join a twice weekly program that uses hip hop to encourage not only reading but writing as well. Enrolment in both programs is high and the demand for them far outstrips the funds available to present them, but there is interest in expanding this program across the United States and Canada.

A major literacy effort in public libraries across North America has traditionally been the annual summer reading club. However, considering how much effort has been expended on the development and delivery of summer reading programs, it is surprising that so little North American research has been done on the effectiveness of these programs. It is probably a safe assumption that the children who do read during the summer retain or increase the comprehension skills and vocabulary that they developed during the school year, and children who don't read during the summer start the school year in September with fewer reading skills than when they left school in June. Still, considering how much staff effort and money is spent on developing summer reading programs there is a need to prove the effectiveness of the programs with quantitative research. Currently, Dominican University's Graduate School of Library and Information Science is conducting a study "Do public library summer reading programs impact student achievement?" The findings from this three-year study are to be made available in 2009. This study is expected to provide information not only on the effectiveness of the summer reading clubs in the 11 communities that participated in the study but also to provide a context for further research.

At the pre-conference session of the American Library Association focusing on summer reading clubs, the Canadian TD Summer Reading Club was discussed along with other cooperative clubs provided in the United States. The TD Summer Reading Club was the envy of many American libraries; the TD Bank Financial Group supplies the funds to provide each child who joins with a poster, an activity booklet to record their reading, and stickers given out as incentives throughout the summer. The artwork used in the program is created by a Canadian illustrator of children's books, which helps promote Canadian books illustrated by local artists. Past illustrators have included Barbara Reid, Robin Muller, Paul Morin, and Ange Zhang. Children are invited to join the club through visits to schools in May and June and invitations sent home with report cards. In addition, a major advertising campaign is launched every June with posters in subways and newspaper ads to encourage parents to bring their children to the public library. In recent years, the TD Summer Reading Club has developed an interactive website on which children can participate either from library computers or from their home or another remote location.

The study "Opening doors to children: Reading, media and public library use by children in six Canadian cities" (2005) provided the opportunity to interview Canadian children for their opinions about summer reading clubs. Children clearly identified that they enjoyed the program and would join again. They also identified that they read more because of membership in the program. The study also provides information on the types of books that boys and girls preferred.

When asked what types of stories they preferred, children clearly identified adventure and mysteries as their favourite types of books, as shown in the following table. This information showed how important it is to choose themes that appealed to both boys and girls in the reading clubs. That is why the themes chosen immediately after the report was written in 2005 have incorporated a mystery or adventure theme. In 2005, a spaceship theme was used with the title *Blast Off*. This was followed by *Quest for Heroes* in 2006 and *Lost Worlds* in 2007. For the summer of 2008, a humour theme was chosen, *Laugh Out Loud* or LOL, in recognition that many children identified "funny stories" as a preference.

Fiction Preferences

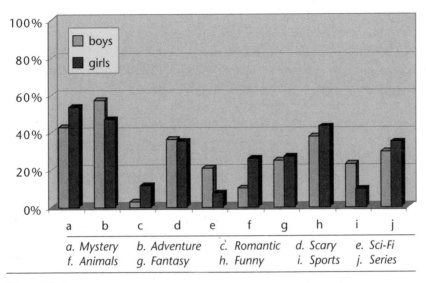

a. Mystery b. Adventure c. Romantic d. Scary e. Sci-Fi
f. Animals g. Fantasy   h. Funny   i. Sports j. Series

Figure 13.1.

    Summer reading clubs are not just about visiting the library, getting posters and logbooks, then reading at home and returning to the library to report on books read. Many clubs also have digital components with a website for children to visit and explore. Needless to say, the sites have many book promotion elements, but there are also games and activities for children to enjoy. On one site, the book reviewing section encourages children to write reviews for the books they have read. The advantage is that children are the best promoters of books—having a peer recommend a book is always more effective than having a review from an unknown source. The spelling and grammar may be lacking, but the enthusiasm is infectious in many of the reviews. Here is one example of the children's reviews:

> *Written by Kathleen* (10)
> *Lizabeth's Story* by Erika Tamar
>
> This is a great story I reccomend for all girls. I was reading it late at night and could hardly put it down!

Such reviews not only promote books but also encourage children to write. Working to increase children's literacy requires that we encourage their writing activities as well.

    Public librarians do as much as they can to encourage children to read by promoting books when visiting schools or childcare centres, providing storytimes and author visits, and providing collections filled with information, imagination, creativity, and excitement. A challenge that children's librarians face in this century, in addition to the rapidly developing technology, is the wealth of new materials published each year. How can one keep up with the massive amount of reading necessary to know the best new materials available? The Internet can help. The shared reading site <*goodreads.com*> provides participants the opportunity to see what others are reading and establish a rapport with a group of readers. It is important for librarians who are trying to encourage reading to belong to their own community of readers.

At the American Library Association's Annual Conference in 2008 the Newbery/Caldecott banquet presented an excellent example of the use of technology in the promotion of books. The winner of the Caldecott award was Brian Selznick for his work *The Invention of Hugo Cabret*. The book is not the traditional 32-page picture book; rather, it looks like a thick, intimidating novel. Readers quickly discover that the story begins simply with illustrated pages and is told through a mix of illustration and text. The book with more than 530 pages is a perfect book for both reluctant and enthusiastic readers. At the awards banquet, Brian Selznick accepted the Caldecott medal after treating the audience to a large-screen broadcast of a new series of illustrations depicting his character receiving the important call announcing his win. His speech which followed the illustrations was wonderful, but greatly overshadowed by the clever use of his art which opened the evening. Promoters of reading can easily find the text of his speech as well as the new illustrations on the Net at Brian Selznick's website or the website for his book. Fans and soon-to-be fans of the book are delighted to find these illustrations and more information about him. Teachers and librarians also introduce children to the movie that inspired Selznick, *A Trip to the Moon* by George Melies, very easily on the Net. The computer can be a most useful reading promotion tool.

Promoting books online has become sophisticated and engaging. Fans of Kenneth Oppel quickly discovered that he uses his website to highlight each of his books and announce new publications. Prior to the release of *Starclimber*, his latest book, his fans could find a great deal of information online about the book. Dramatic music and stunning visuals draw fans and future fans into the worlds that he has created in his books. Librarians who used to deliver booktalks to promote books can now use these sophisticated promotional tools, created specifically for the book with the child audience in mind, when promoting books to readers.

Public libraries will continue to provide services to children as they move into the next hundred years of service. The massive technological advances assist librarians in working with children and the larger community to build a more literate society.

REFERENCE

Fasick, Adele, et al. 2005. *Opening doors to children: Reading, media and public library use in six Canadian cities.* Regina: Regina Public Library.

RESOURCES

Websites (accessed March 31, 2009)

Book Pals: <http://www.bookpals.net/storyline.html>

E-Stories at Enoch Pratt Free Library: <http://www.prattlibrary.org/home/storyIndex.aspx>

Every Child Ready to Read: <http://www.ala.org/ala/mgrp>

Good Reads: <http://www.goodreads.com>

International Children's Digital Library: <http://www.icdlbooks.org/>

TD Summer Reading Club: <http://tdsrc.torontopubliclibrary.ca/>

TPL's KidsSpace: <http://kidsspace.torontopubliclibrary.ca/>

Chapter 14

Rare Books in the Classroom! Interactive Programs and Digital Collections of Historical Children's Books

Leslie McGrath

Special collections of children's books, once seen as the sole preserve of the adult scholar, now offer young students virtual access to the world of very old children's books and book history. There are complete books and manuscripts available online. Some are brought to students onscreen with turn-the-page technology, others with amusing and informative annotations built into the images, and still others offering translations into many languages. There are webquests, self-contained web-based programs with curriculum-support activities or curriculum-based content, some of which might include a variety of digitized primary and secondary research materials, complete with teacher packages developed by experts. I provide here only a brief selection of the impressive resources available today, but they reveal the scope of the sophisticated digital collections and programs that provide a free, multidisciplinary resource for students and teachers alike.

Why study early stories?

From era to era, stories for children range from overtly religious and didactic works through contrived moral and sentimental tales, imaginative works, and perhaps most interesting of all, historical works that tell different versions of past events. Educators have asserted that "Historical fiction and non fiction give children the opportunity to explore alternative viewpoints, examine human conflict and immerse themselves in detailed character studies," (Roser and Keehn 2002, in Chick 2006). The examination of contemporary literature and instructional works through digital collections can further enhance the learning experience.

Today's student is bombarded daily with conflicting messages from various media, in a volume not experienced by earlier generations. Developing the skills of critical analysis and evaluation has never been more important, and there is no more instructive tool than printed texts, both fiction and nonfiction. The passing of years, indeed generations, brings differing viewpoints, and new interpretations of historical developments—and of stories. That today's stories may be seen in new ways in the future, and that we are looking through a contemporary lens that will change according to the viewer and the context, is one of the most useful lessons students can learn. In speaking of Toronto Public Library's Osborne Collection of Early Children's Books, Tim Gauntley, Program Coordinator of Library and Learning Resources and Interdisciplinary Studies, Toronto District School Board, comments:

> I have found the Osborne Collection to be a valuable resource for supporting school library programs and student visits. Students have reported a growing interest in the history and wonder of children's literature, and a particular appreciation for the Osborne's ability to connect with their contemporary reading interests. Teachers have reported a delight at the breadth of the collection and its relationship to curricular issues such as multiculturalism and character education. To now have access to items from this and other special collections online, as well as to curriculum support projects like Ontario History Quest, will make historical materials more accessible than ever before. I will be promoting the incorporation of this material and the rich insights it offers to young lives into school library work and such courses as history, literature, family studies, and interdisciplinary studies. (Gauntley 2008)

Online advantages

There is more to be gained than research skills, analytical skills, and historical facts. A wide range of multidisciplinary studies is supported by looking at early artifacts, manuscripts, and books. What are really old children's books like? How did book illustration develop? How did printing change over time? What is censorship? Such questions, together with subject-specific information on children's literature, authors, and publishers can be found in the digital collections and programs.

New multilingual digital collections also offer access to the same story in a wide variety of languages, allowing children, particularly those newly arrived in a country and dealing with unfamiliar concepts, to share the experience of a story, to gain understanding more quickly, and to enjoy books in their mother tongue even if hard-copy texts are unavailable.

Finally, there is the enjoyment of collaborative research projects using online resources. Socialization and collaboration have been proven to increase achievement in elementary students, including at-risk students (Chick 2006).

The workplace reality that many students will eventually enter requires collaborative work to resolve problems. Some of the projects outlined below offer fully developed curriculum packages for group activities that build participants' communication and presentation skills in a collegial, supportive environment. Some of the projects offer choices for individual or group activities. What they all have in common is based on the oldest educational rule of all—the most effective learning tools are those that work "with the grain," using tools the children enjoy to combine valuable learning with priceless fun.

When writing about the improvements needed to make history a more popular subject among Canadian schoolchildren, Douglas Gosse recommends giving students a sense of participation in past events through collaborative activities and role-playing (Gosse 2003). What could give a greater sense of being part of the story than an interactive game in which young students become Empire Loyalists and must make life-and-death choices to survive and thrive in the pioneer land to which they escape? Such activities may provide the context that will assist a student to progress to reading full-length historical fiction.

Sources of information

Although the information in this chapter is accurate at the time of writing, access points and the content of digital programs and resources can quickly change. If you find that a URL does not work, use a general search engine such as Google to find the institution listed, then a keyword search of the site to find the program listing. Sponsors of each digital program are listed on the websites. The list is organized by name of institution, then by subject heading of all the resources. Asterisks mark the resources designed for children. Some examples of virtual exhibitions from collections of rare children's books are appended.

Websites accessed March 31, 2009

Library and Archives Canada
Title: Children's Literature Service**
Website: <http://www.collectionscanada.gc.ca/childrenliterature/index-e.html>
Description: The Children's Literature Service of the National Library of Canada provides a portal to eleven Special Collections of Children's Literature in Canada, a few of which currently offer digital resources.

Canadian National Catalogue
Website: <http://www.collectionscanada.gc.ca/amicus/index-e.html>
Description: AMICUS is a free catalogue listing the holdings of libraries across Canada. As a national catalogue, AMICUS not only shows the published materials held at Library and Archives Canada (LAC) but also those located in over 1300 libraries across Canada. AMICUS contains over 30 million records

for books, magazines, newspapers, government documents, theses, sound recordings, maps, electronic texts as well as items in Braille and large print. *Also check out:* <http://www.collectionscanada.gc.ca/pika/index-e.html>

American Antiquarian Society
Title: Teach us History
Website: <http://teachushistory.org/>
Description: A website for older students, developed by the American Antiquarian Society, that contains primary source materials, lesson plans, and background essays that examine critical developments in American history. Subjects include the American Revolution, the Civil War, and the War of 1812, among others; the coverage features interactive classroom activities such as audio and film clips.

Baldwin Library of Children's Literature, Digital Collections, University of Florida
Titles: Afterlife of Alice and Her Adventures in Wonderland, Daniel Defoe's "Robinson Crusoe" & the Robinsonades, *St. Nicholas* Magazine
Website: <http://www.uflib.ufl.edu/UFDC/?c=juv>
Description: Full-text digital collections of particular strengths in one of the foremost collections of American and British Children's Literature, including five digitized books related to *Alice in Wonderland*, 192 full-text versions of *Robinson Crusoe* and *Robinsonades*, and a virtually complete digital collection of the first 23 volumes of *St. Nicholas* Magazine, which was widely read in both the United States and Canada, and to which many Canadian authors, such as Lucy Maud Montgomery, contributed spanning the years 1873–1897.

This project was funded in part by the National Endowment for the Humanities (NEH).

de Grummond Children's Literature Collection, McCain Library, University of Southern Mississippi
Titles: The Cinderella Project, The Red Riding Hood Project, Jack and the Beanstalk/Jack the Giant Killer Project
Websites: <http://www.usm.edu/english/fairytales/cinderella/cinderella.html> <http://www.usm.edu/english/fairytales/lrrh/lrrhhome.htm>, <http://www.usm.edu/English/fairytales/jack/jackhome.html>
Description: Designed by Dr. Michael Salda, these projects are text and image archives that contain various versions of the fairy tales that can be printed from the site, for "reconstruction" of the books, together with background materials and resource listings. This material is made available free for non-profit educational use, provided Dr. Salda's projects are credited as the source. The "Cinderella" website has 12 English-language versions, and "The Little Red Riding Hood" site has 16 English-language versions, dated 1700–1900. The "Jack and the Beanstalk" site offers nine English-language versions of the story, together with games material.

Hamilton Public Library, Kingston-Frontenac Public Library, and Toronto Public Library

Title: The Ontario Time Machine: Really Old Ontario Books (OTM) **
Website: <http://www.ontariotimemachine.ca/>
Description: This is a curriculum-connected rather than curriculum-based project that offers engaging support for historical studies. There is a teacher's guide describing a unit that will span several lessons and class periods, and its recommended evaluation plan will engage teachers of history, language, as well as the teacher-librarian, creating a multidisciplinary approach. The OTM offers cooperative group or individual study opportunities. Stocked with items from major Ontario libraries, the project contains 31 historical books suitable for study by grade 7 and 8 students, and is designed to operate within a closed Internet environment (i.e., complete except for a few external website links). The project, which features turn-the-page technology and links, was funded in part by the Ontario Ministry of Culture and the Canadian Culture Online Program of Canadian Heritage, Library and Archives Canada, and the Canadian Council of Archives.

Figure 14.1. The Ontario Time Machine website

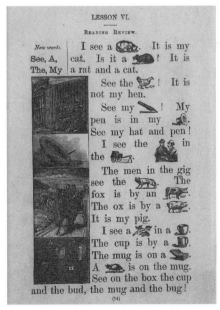

Figure 14.2. Page from *First Reader, Part 1*

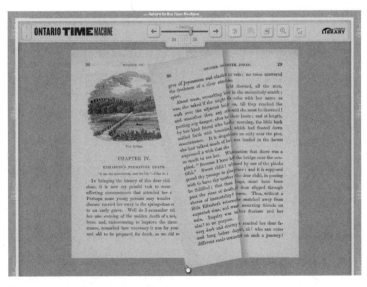

Figure 14.3. The OTM turn-the-page technology

Hockliffe Collection of Children's Books, De Montfort University
Title: The Hockliffe Project
Website: <http://www.cts.dmu.ac.uk/AnaServer?hockliffe+0+start.anv>
Description: The Hockliffe Collection, owned by De Montfort University, consists of over 1,000 early children's books, ranging in date from 1685 to the mid-twentieth century. Hockliffe Project was created and its web presence is maintained at De Montfort University. It is intended to provide access to holdings and to encourage research in early English children's literature. The site is not designed for young students, but if one needs a digitized early version of a particular children's book title—from Isaac Watts's *Divine Songs*, 1715, to a chapbook of *Seven Champions of Christendom*, 1801—it is likely to be found in the Hockliffe Project. Funding for the project was provided by the Arts and Humanities Research Board.

International Children's Digital Library
Title: International Children's Digital Library **
Website: <http://www.icdlbooks.org/>
Description: Early and modern books (3,745 books as of March 21, 2009) in a wide range of languages (51) are fully digitized with clear text (enlargement) and pop-forward options. Originally created by an interdisciplinary research team at the University of Maryland in cooperation with the Internet Archive, this project is especially designed, with the help of a team of children, for outstanding user-friendliness. Since its launch in 2002, over a million people have visited the website—most popular item is an early alphabet book, *A—Apple Pie*. The mission of ICDL is stated on its website: "to excite and inspire the world's children to become members of the global community—children who understand the value of tolerance and respect for diverse cultures, languages and ideas—by making the best in children's literature available online." [1]

Université Laval
Title: Les manuels scolaires québécois, Université Laval
Website: <http://www.bibl.ulaval.ca/ress/manscol/>
Description: A collection of digitized sample pages from French- and English-language early schoolbooks, from a collection of texts dating from 1765,

---

[1] See also the University of Minnesota's Kerlan Collection Books Online, <http://special.lib.umn.edu/clrc/kerlan/index.php> for full text images of *Songs of Father Goose*, *Dot and Tot of Merryland*, *The Enchanted Isle of Yew*, *The Adventures of Santa Claus* and more, scanned as a contribution to the University of Maryland's International Children's Digital Library project, and specialized Kerlan resources such as The Censorship Portfolio, found by scrolling down the main page of Kerlan Collection listings: <http://special.lib.umn.edu/clrc/kerlan/>

"Censorship" is one of the teacher-support packages that offers an intriguing contrast to well-known resources on censorship in Canada, and will be useful for Canadian students. Young Americans express their opinions about censorship; links connect the portfolio to ALA's lists of the most frequently-challenged children's books in the United States in the past ten years, author viewpoints, statements from civil rights groups and more.

mainly published or printed in Quebec. This is a university catalogue, not designed for children's use, but older students will find the thematic list of illustrations from early children's books useful. For example, choosing the theme "chat" brings images of cats from *Le livre des enfans* [sic], Quebec: T. Cary, 1834, p.14 and from William Mavor's *The English spelling book*, from the 241st London edition, Montreal: H.H. Cummingham, 1837.[2]

Children's Collections, Lilly Library, Indiana University, Bloomington
Title: Jane Johnson Manuscript Nursery Library
Website: <http://www.indiana.edu/~liblilly/collections.html>
Description: A digital collection of materials created by Jane (Russell) Johnson (1706–1759) for her children, including her son George William Johnson (1740?–1814), who became High Sheriff of Lincolnshire in 1784. The materials consist of alphabet cards, lesson cards, and verses, 438 items in all, arranged in 24 groups. Many of the verses are mounted on Dutch flowery paper. The Lilly Library contains the Elisabeth Ball Collection with over 10,000 holdings, including an extensive collection of chapbooks (small booklets) and rare children's books. This site is not designed for children's use, but it offers intriguing examples of handmade home-schooling materials created by a careful parent in the eighteenth century.

The Rosetta Project
Title: Children's Books Online **
Website: <http://www.childrensbooksonline.org/>
Description: Established in 1996, this is possibly the largest online collection of full-text, downloadable early children's texts (18th to 20th century) available today. Many of the texts have been translated into numerous languages. A number of the books can be listened to in audio recordings, also available in multiple languages. The scope of the project is made possible by the fact that it is staffed entirely by volunteers, and that contributions and translations are gathered from around the world. This is a very attractive site that children will enjoy using.

Toronto Public Library
Title: Curator's Choice Digital manuscript: "The Sad Tale of Mrs. Mole and Mrs. Mouse"
Website: <http://ve.torontopubliclibrary.ca/showcase/showcase.html>
Description: Toronto Public Library's digitized collections are growing. One especially intriguing item from the Osborne Collection of Early Children's Books is the manuscript "The Sad Tale of Mrs. Mole and Mrs. Mouse,"

---

[2] Some references are made in this website to texts digitized by the Canadian Institute for Historical Microreproductions (CIHM), now Early Canadiana Online, <http://www.canadiana.org/eco.php>, produced by Canadiana.org with the support of Library and Archives Canada, Canadian Heritage and other sponsors. This site is designed for adult use, and contains complete texts of research documents.

written and illustrated for her four-year-old daughter by Jane Vaughan Cotton, of the de Montizambert family of Montreal, *ca.* 1849. Annotated by Osborne librarians, it provides definitions and explanations for unfamiliar terms and activities. The Osborne Collection of Early Children's Books is a research collection, primarily in English, of books, book-related art, archives, and ephemera, to which children are welcome visitors. See <http://www.torontopubliclibrary.ca> under "Collections."

Toronto Public Library
Title: Ontario History Quest **
Website: <http://ohq.torontopubliclibrary.ca> (accessed March 31, 2009).
Description: Another TPL online project is *Ontario History Quest* (OHQ), a collaborative project in which curriculum-supported history programs for grades 7, 8, 10, and 12 guide students through the basics of historical thematic research on curriculum-centred topics, using webquests (inquiry-oriented activities for online student research, including the standard elements of task, process, evaluation and conclusion, and appendices). Developed in consultation with an education specialist, the project is a classroom-ready student resource that meets the Ontario Ministry of Education curriculum expectations for grades 7, 8, 10, and 12, and includes a teacher package for each grade.

The teacher packages include time required for activities, teaching and learning strategies, curriculum expectations, evaluation rubrics, and preparatory checklists. This program is designed for users ranging from novice to professional, and for home or classroom use. OHQ is not composed of children's books, but of research materials accessible to children in the appropriate grade range, with accompanying reading lists. The project also includes complementary access to the OHQ digital collections with over 4,400 images captured and indexed from the Archives of Ontario, the City of Toronto Archives, and Toronto Public Library, covering periods 1780s-1820s, 1820s-1850s, 1890s-1920s and 1945-1970s, with keyword and Boolean searching possible, together with categories such as place names and formats (maps, diaries).

Phase 2 of this project, which will include the interactive Empire Loyalist game on the adventures of a Loyalist family escaping to Canada, plus a French-language site for grade 7 will be launched in fall 2009.

Conclusion

All online projects and digital collections lead back to the Special Collections, the homes of the books. Through virtual access, students have an opportunity to study artifacts of the past and to broaden their interests; as well, they learn to create their own stories, historical studies, and interpretations. In general, only a small percentage of library holdings can appear in elaborate presentations. Such projects are designed to encourage interest and further exploration, which can include contacting curators to learn more about the collections from which particular images are drawn. Librarians are accessible by email and can provide information resources for teachers and teacher-librarians, and in the particular case of public libraries, to assist patrons of every age with research in and enjoyment of library resources.

REFERENCES

Chick, Kay A. 2006. "Fostering student collaboration through the use of historical texts." *The Social Studies*. July–Aug., 152–7.

Gauntley, Tim. Letter to Leslie McGrath, September 9, 2008. Osborne Collection of Early Children's Books, Toronto Public Library.

Gosse, Douglas. 2003. "History methods for all." *School Libraries in Canada*. 22.3, 12–3.

Roser, Nancy and Susan Keehn. 2002. "Fostering thought, talk, inquiry: Linking literature and social studies." *Reading Teacher* 55, 416–26. Quoted in the article by Kay A. Chick.

Library Subject Guide

LITERATURE
Full text collections
Children's Books Online (Rosetta Project)
The Hockliffe Project (de Montfort University)
International Children's Digital Library (ICDL, University of Maryland)

Special Projects—*Fairy Tales*
The Cinderella Project (de Grummond Children's Literature Collection, University of South Mississippi)
Jack and the Beanstalk/ Jack the Giant Killer Project (de Grummond Children's Literature Collection, University of South Mississippi)
The Red Riding Hood Project (de Grummond Children's Literature Collection, University of South Mississippi)

Special Projects—*Literature*
Afterlife of Alice and Her Adventures in Wonderland (Baldwin Library of Historical Children's Literature, University of Florida)
Daniel Defoe's Robinson Crusoe and the Robinsonnades (Baldwin Library of Historical Children's Literature, University of Florida)

Special Projects—*Periodicals*
St. Nicholas Magazine (Baldwin Library of Historical Children's Literature, University of Florida)

Special Projects—*Poetry*

"The Sad Tale of Mrs. Mole and Mrs. Mouse," (Osborne Collection of Early Children's Books, Toronto Public Library)

HISTORY

History—*Ontario*

Ontario History Quest (Toronto Public Library, Archives of Ontario, City of Toronto Archives)

Ontario Time Machine (Kingston Frontenac Public Library, Hamilton Public Library and Toronto Public Library)

History—United States

TeachUSHistory.org (American Antiquarian Association)

EDUCATION

Instructional works—*Manuscripts*

Jane Johnson Nursery Manuscripts Library (Kerlan Collection, University of Minnesota)

Instructional works—*French language*

Les manuels scolaires québécois (Université Laval)

VIRTUAL EXHIBITIONS (SAMPLE LIST)

"The Magic Lantern," Cotsen's Children's Library, Princeton University<http://ccl.princeton.edu/> Describes the technology of early projection devices, and offers an attractive visual presentation based on authentic hand-painted slides.

The Cotsen Children's Library at Princeton is one of America's major historical collections of illustrated children's books, art and educational toys. The site also offers three other virtual exhibitions. See also the Cotsen virtual exhibitions, "Water babies, Creepy-Crawlies" and "Beatrix Potter."

"All Aboard Toronto! Railways and the Growth of a City." Toronto Public Library's Special Collections. Includes a "Train Tour," "Online Gallery" and Fun and Games" for children, with authentic sound clips and activities. <http://ve.torontopubliclibrary.ca/allaboard/>

"The Art of Children's Picture Book Illustration" and other exhibitions, Library and Archives Canada—check through <http://www.collectionscanada.gc.ca>

Also provides access to "ABCs at Play—Beyond the Letters: A Retrospective of Canadian Alphabet Books - Library and Archives Canada." Materials are largely contemporary; sponsorship provided by the Canadian Culture Online Program.

"This Magical Book." Nine moving images from an exhibition of movable books at The Osborne Collection of Early Children's Books, Toronto Public Library, 2002.
<http://ve.torontopubliclibrary.ca/magicbook/home.html>

See also the virtual tour of "Picture Perfect! Canadian children's book illustration." Enter the exhibition through a display of picture-book cave art, and take a regional tour of favourite picture book illustrations from across the country, <http://ve.torontopubliclibrary.ca/PicturePerfect/main.html>

"Pop-Up and Movable Books" from the University of North Texas. <http://www.library.unt.edu/rarebooks/exhibits/popup2/introduction.htm>

Tucked into this exhibit are pop-up images that the student will enjoy as well as activities like dressing Fuller paper dolls in various outfits.

Section Six

Afterword

Chapter 15

Children's Literature and the New Literacies: What about assessment?

Shelley Stagg Peterson

If a literacy task of any sort is worth doing in a classroom, then we should provide feedback to students on how well they achieve the goals of the task. I think most teachers would agree with this. After putting their heart into a task, students eagerly look forward to our perspective on how well they have achieved their purpose. Or if they have struggled, students appreciate feedback that shows what they can do to be more successful. And so, if we truly believe that the teaching practices outlined in this book are worthwhile, we need to consider carefully how we're going to assess students' learning as they engage with the new literacies texts.

How might assessment look in new literacies classrooms? I believe that it won't be radically different. We'll expand on what we already do to take a broader view of students as literacy learners and social beings who use print, digital technologies, and multimedia to communicate with and learn from others. We'll build on the tools and practices that have always been regarded as effective assessment practices. Portfolios of student work, observation checklists, and student-teacher conferences, for example, have a built-in flexibility that makes them ideal for new literacies classrooms. The rubrics, checklists, and scoring guides that have evolved as we have come to know how children learn still have a place. We'll simply expand the criteria to include the processes and products of new literacies. Broadening our assessment means recognizing two new considerations—the demands on students' thinking and decision-making processes, and the demands on their flexibility in adapting to new social communication contexts.

Recognizing thinking and decision-making processes

In a new literacies classroom, I observed one group of students in the process of creating a PowerPoint of photographs, drawings, and text that showed what they had learned about how cat litter and dry pet food are made—they were doing these activities after reading Bill Slavin's *Transformed: How Everyday Things Are Made* (2005). Another group created a Facebook page for fifteen-year-old Kaleigh Wyse, the protagonist in Shelley Hrdlitschka's *Sun Signs* (2005), who writes emails to her online teacher and classmates in a correspondence course she takes while undergoing cancer treatments. Yet another group conducted an online literature discussion group with students from another school in the province as they shared their responses to Christopher Paul Curtis's *Elijah of Buxton* (2007). The overall goals of the digital or multimodal response activities—to deepen students' understandings and enhance their experiences with the texts—were no different from those of any literature response activity. The goals had been expanded, however, in keeping with the communication possibilities and demands of modern texts.

Students' thinking and composing processes require more than determining which words to use and how to put them together in a coherent way, and our assessment must acknowledge the complex decision making involved. Our assessment should recognize that students have made decisions in selecting appropriate images, in determining the optimal number of images to make their point, and in creating an appealing layout for their audience. Our assessment should take into account students' decision making about the message they are sending by using particular camera angles, for example, recognizing that looking down at the object makes it seem less powerful or significant. They must consider what sizes the images should be in relation to each other in order to show the relative importance, strength, and power of parts of each image. They also should anticipate how readers' and viewers' attention will shift between words and pictures and how they might go from web page to web page using hyperlinks to gather the needed information from the digital texts. Assessing students' thinking processes could take the form of conversations in student-teacher conferences, students' written self-assessments of their processes, teachers' informal observations while students work on their digital or multimedia texts, or tracing the decision making when marking the texts themselves. When assessing the digital or multimedia products, it is important to consider how students use the text forms to achieve their purposes.

Considerations of the interplay of print, visual, and sound information are as important for students when reading, viewing, and listening to digital and multimedia texts as they are when creating these texts. In order to deepen their understanding of these texts, students make meaning not only of the words but also of the images and sounds, and of the relationships between all of these information sources. To understand students' reading processes, teachers' questions in student-teacher conferences and their observations of students' discussions of digital and multimedia texts should consider the students' use of the various types of information and their relationships to each other.

Plagiarism is an issue when students create digital and multimedia responses to literature. With abandon, students search websites, copying and pasting texts and images or downloading sounds and music, mashing them together to create something that is unique in some respects because it brings together bits and pieces that have not previously been integrated into one text. Nonetheless, the bits and pieces were someone else's creations in their original forms. Students' decision-making processes should be assessed in terms of how they have made the original bits their own and whether they have credited the original creators of the bits. Beyond this, however, lies the issue of how students' learning can be assessed when much of their digital and multimedia work creations come from the inspiration and hard work of someone else. This issue warrants deeper discussion than is possible here, of course, but I raise it for teachers' consideration when determining how to assess digital and multimedia products.

Recognizing how students deal with demands of the social contexts

Often, students' digital and multimedia responses to literature have a much wider audience than a handwritten response in a reader response journal that will be read only by their teacher and, possibly, by another student if it is a buddy journal. The audience is unknown to students who respond through wikis or blogs or through creating digital collages with poetry and images that are displayed in a local community centre or art gallery as in Mary Ladky's and Miriam Davidson's chapter, for example. As a result, the assignment is more challenging. Students cannot make assumptions about what their audience knows and has experienced, and they must include text and visual information that is accessible to the wider audience. Correspondingly, our assessment of the products that students create should consider how well students have responded to this broader demand on their communication abilities, how they have used print and design conventions appropriate to the social context. Again, students' self-assessments and student-teacher conferences are helpful in finding out from students, themselves, how their sense of their audience has influenced their decision making.

We could also consider how students adapt their writing processes to meet the demands of the situation. For example, when writing a narrative to accompany a photo story as part of the Cyberwriters project that Jen Thompson writes about, students would likely spend more time planning, seeking out, and organizing information than they would if they were writing a story about a humorous event that happened to them last year. They also might spend more time revising to cut unnecessary words because there might be length restrictions to ensure that all students have equal space on the CD-ROM, whereas the story has no limits on its length.

The collaborative work that is encouraged in digital forums such as wikis presents the same issues that any collaborative projects do, because everyone who participates gets credit for the final product, regardless of their contributions. Although the goal is for all students to learn from each other, with everyone's contributions being valued, there is a chance that some students will choose not to contribute and that others may dominate and override their peers' contributions. Wikis provide a means for teachers to trace the contributions of all participants, and teachers are encouraged to use this feature when assessing wiki and other collaborative projects. Students' thinking and revising processes are captured in a concrete form for teachers. Students can also provide a self-assessment of their contributions to ensure greater individual accountability.

Assessing the authority of texts and possible social or political agendas that their authors may have, always a part of interpreting print texts, is particularly important when reading digital and multimedia texts. It is far easier to post a text on the Internet than it is to have a piece published in a book, newspaper, or magazine. With no editors to satisfy, Internet contributors can more readily post texts with inaccuracies or a strong bias. Students' critical reading processes should be considered when assessing students' reading in new literacies classrooms. Students must determine the authority and perspectives of the creators of the texts they read as they compare and contrast information from various sources to determine which is most accurate.

Assessment as learning opportunity for students and teachers

Assessment should be an important part of conversations about children's literature and new literacies. We need to consider how to provide feedback that will enhance students' learning as they engage with these various texts. We miss out on valuable teaching opportunities when we do not carry out any assessments to provide students with feedback, or when we assess using tools and practices that were meant for literacy activities with less complex communication and design demands. To grow as literacy learners in modern times, students need to receive feedback that recognizes their success in addressing these broader demands.

In classrooms where new literacies and children's literature are brought together, assessment can be as exciting as the teaching and learning possibilities that have been described in this book. Through our observations of students as they interact with texts, through our oral and written conversations with students as they reflect on their thinking and decision-making processes, and through expanding the criteria used to assess new literacies products, we capture the richness of students' learning in new literacies classrooms. We discover how our students deal with the demands of ever-widening social situations where the world is a potential audience for their print, visual, and aural compositions, and where they have access to a world of ideas through Internet texts. Our assessment practices are our learning opportunities as we work alongside our students with the ever-expanding array of digital, media, and print texts that are available to us.

REFERENCES

Curtis, Christopher Paul. 2007. *Elijah of Buxton*. Toronto: Scholastic Canada.

Hrdlitschka, Shelley. 2005. *Sun Signs*. Vancouver, BC: Orca Book Publishers.

Slavin, Bill. 2005. *Transformed: How everyday things are made*. Toronto: Kids Can Press.

Chapter 16

Read Me a Story, But Plug it in First!
David Booth

This book is full of truly significant articles examining the effects of the new world of technology on the old world of children's literature, and these writers have opened up so many conversations for me, both in my head as I confront my own assumptions and biases and with colleagues about how we can help teachers who feel like immigrants arriving in the new world without knowledge of the language or the geography. Are we frightened or excited by the technology? homesick for the reading nook? or full of adventurous spirit? Are we railing against the wireless connections? clutching our book bags? or putting a new battery in our digital mouse? Or all of the above some of the time? What if we, as readers, have been part of the journey all along, but unaware of all the new directions we were taking? Have we been involved with technology in unknown ways? How do we define technology? How will we redefine a book? And just what will or should our children experience in the future under the category of Children's Literature? And will the text we love smell of library paste or light up in the darkness? We may need to ask Alice in Wonderland for some answers.

As I read each chapter, I was nudged into remembering the texts of my childhood—books and comics and radio programs and movies and sermons and, eventually, television. Each medium different, but part of the whole of my life; the intertextuality of my childhood. I remember that, as a child, when Dr. Seuss's *How the Grinch Stole Christmas* (1957) was reprinted in a women's magazine, I ripped it out along the perforated edges, delighting in my ownership of a book for free. And last year, the *Hamilton Spectator* newspaper published a chapter a week of a children's novel by Jerry Spinelli.

Do you remember the filmstrips from elementary school—sometimes images and text from a real book, not just a sequence from nature study? Or a filmed version of a classic children's novel, *The Count of Monte Cristo* (Dumas

1844–46), or *Treasure Island* (Stevenson, 1883)? I loved knowing that a book I had loved could be re-experienced on screen, in Technicolor! In grades 3 and 4, I read every fairy tale book in the public library, dwelling on those with the coloured plates, where artists from a century or two before had created their painted tapestries of the stories, lush and fantastical and sensuous, to remind us of the magical truth of the tales.

Is *Pinocchio* (Collodi 1883) a children's book? When I was eight, my Aunt Bert took me to see the film at the movie theatre, but we left half way through; she had become bored with it, so for me, the story is indeed a cultural reference, but without an ending. The maligning of Disney films, of what we called children's literature icons, seems a waste of time; for millions of children and adults, the film is the tale, just as when I ask teachers to describe for me the characteristics of the lawyer in the book *To Kill a Mockingbird* (Lee 1960), and they always shout out "Gregory Peck." We need to remain vigilant so that our critiques of the formats of literature for children do not damage treasured memories. Popular literature, defined primarily as that which has first appeared as part of a television show, cartoon series, or film, packs a mighty wallop. Judging popularity and quality is always a minefield.

Recently in New York, I had the opportunity to view a display of William Steig's artwork, illustrations from his many picture books, and a biographical film of his life. He would have been one hundred years old in November 2007. I learned so much about him and his magical work from that visit—some of the displays were technologically interactive, by the way. I remember *Caleb and Kate* (1986), *Brave Irene* (1986), *Abel's Island* (1985), and *Amos and Boris* (1992), and there they all were, hanging in front of me, all at once. Not in books, but on walls. Without printed text. And then I entered a small room that contained all of the drawings from the animated film *Shrek*. What a shock to my system. All of these images on transparencies, so far from my medium of the picture book, my treasured modality, and yet bringing delight to the children who were moving from visual to visual, at home with their friendly objects taken from the film. For Christmas, I gave my five-year-old nephew Frankie a *Shrek* kit—a DVD, a book, and a stuffed toy. I was a stranger in his town, but William Steig had become his neighbour.

How today's children interact with texts, both in print form and on screen, has changed the nature of children's literature and has generated new forms and combinations of texts. However, Len Unsworth (2006) says that what we are seeing is not a replacement of books per se but "strongly synergistic complementaries, where the story worlds of books are extended and enhanced by various forms of digital multimedia and, correspondingly, some types of digital narratives frequently have companion publications in book form."

We need to think about the relationships among the new digital texts and the familiar, traditional book forms. Unsworth gives us three categories to help us frame the discussion:

- Augmented literary texts where online resources enhance and extend the book (such as the extras we find at the end of every movie DVD that we rent)
- Recontextualized literacy texts, scanned onto CD-ROMs, or animated, or presented in audio versions
- Originated literary texts, published in digital formats only, including narratives, images, and hypertext variations. (Of course, some of these are then transposed into book forms.)

We now have e-books, e-magazines, e-stories, e-comics, e-information, and e-poems, not to mention e-video games, the most popular of the texts designed and created for children. Reading has now been redefined to include making meaning with a variety of text forms, or combinations of forms. But then, we have known about the complexities of this term *reading* for many years, as James Moffett told us in 1976. Children will continue to experience print, graphics, and sounds interrelated and interconnected as different dimensions of children's literature.

We know that the students' engagement with text can be extended and deepened through response activities, and that these can incorporate the multimodal forms that surround the children in their lives as they explore the author's content, structure, and forms by interpreting, constructing, and representing their own ideas and emotions in a variety of modes. The children then become the *text makers*, expressing and sharing their constructs with others so that their texts beget other texts. We might call these new forms *informal* children's literature, as we recognize the power of the peer creation as a force for literacy in the classroom. Children are then developing an awareness of how different texts work, from the inside out, learning that all the new forms are a valuable resource in developing their own interpretations, their narratives, their new-found information, or their word play. After all, a crayon is certainly a technological tool, whether it be a wax Crayola or a mouse-driven colour brush on screen.

I am on my computer, involved with issues of children's literature and literacy, every day. At night, I carry home my laptop, alongside my books, in my case. There are hundreds, even thousands, of websites devoted to children's books—for those of us who want to be aware of new publications in different countries; for those of us who want to investigate the theory and practice of children's books; for those of us who want information, historical or contemporary, about the books, the authors and illustrators, or the context for their creation; for those of us who want to find activities for engaging with the whole experience; for those of us who want to chat with others about the world of children's literature; but, in this new world, especially for those of us who want to experience the literature texts online, on handheld readers, on iPods, on phones. Jean Little, the well-known Canadian author, can't go to sleep without reading a good book—through her ears, since she is blind. Technology has always been her colleague in children's literature. My mother's favourite singer was Marian Anderson, and I was touched deeply as I read the book *When Marian Sang* (Ryan 2002; also available on Kindle), but even more emotionally connected when I watched the video of her singing at the Lincoln Memorial on the website Marian Anderson: A Life in Song. My mother would have enjoyed both of these texts.

Walter Dean Myers's website opened up a new world for me as a teacher—I just now googled his name and 1,010,000 entries appeared on screen. Gone were the blackboard notes about Charles Dickens, laboriously copied by hand with bits of chalk, to be later replicated by youngsters with bits of pencil. Now students can find Mem Fox's biographical information alongside her thoughts on reading and writing, read the questions and answers on Avi's homepage, and be warned by Lemony Snicket: "If I were you, I would immediately turn your computer off rather than view any of the dreadful images, read any of the wretched information, play any of the unnerving games or examine the unpleasant books presented within this web site." Or they could read *Beatrice's Goat* by Page McBrier, a story of a young girl who can attend school because of her family's receiving an income-producing goat, and then visit the *Heifer Project* online, the international organization that gives gifts of cattle, sheep, rabbits, guinea pigs, honeybees, pigs, llamas, water buffalo, camels, alpacas, yaks, horses, chicks, ducks, goats, geese, fish, other regionally appropriate livestock, as well as tree seedlings, to those in need. As of 2006, these animals and plants have been distributed in more than 125 countries around the globe, promoting agroecology and sustainability. Children can see a photo of the real Beatrice, and even raise funds to buy a goat for another family. A book can generate hope for a world, and technology can give birth to a goat for a village.

The International Children's Digital Library has created a freely available online library of outstanding children's books from all over the world. The current collection that is available without cost over the Internet includes more than 1600 books in 38 languages. Its mandate is to connect the right book to the right child at the right time, and this is all now possible through technology. This organization has become a storyteller for McLuhan's global village. And what does a book look like now, pray tell?

My nine-month old granddaughter is sitting on my lap as I read to her *Goodnight Moon* (Brown 2001), the board book version, which she has happily been sucking on for half an hour. She is wearing slippers modelled on the ones in the book, and she toys with the bunny heads on them as she looks at each of the pictures. My own copy of the book is a dog-eared paperback, and I enjoy the sturdy feel of the pages of this new text format as I read. (Look—there's a CD-ROM attached to the back cover with the story being read by a film star). My colleague Shelley Peterson suggests that there will soon be picture books with built-in Internet connections so that, as I turn a page, all kinds of related texts will be made available to support my reading of this story—perhaps the phases of the moon or images of children in different places in the world getting ready for sleep. Each time, a new telling will emerge from the intertextuality of the components, but then, that also happens with only the paper text, the words and images, and the adult's voice—each time, a new story. Will *Goodnight Moon* become a pop-up book with an infinite number of flaps to open into the moon-lighted night?

These things I know because this book has told me so—I will read my books in print or online or through my iPod. I will scan the Internet in search of the warmth and support my community of children's literature lovers will continue to offer me. I will read to children, talk with them about what they are reading in whatever text form they enjoy. I will attempt to expand their worlds through searches on the Internet, through my life stories, through conversations with others who have experienced the same text, through composing and constructing our responses to the thoughts and emotions the text-makers have generated. I will attempt to honour their homes, their cultures, their religions, their genders with texts that illuminate and challenge their lives. Children will continue to love conversation, story, song, poetry, pictures, images, information, biographies, and games, all of the texts in all of the forms that can help develop them, like magical pieces of Lego, into the citizens we dream they will become.

REFERENCES

Brown, Margaret Wise. 2001. *Goodnight Moon*. Originally published 1947. Available from New York: HarperCollins.

Collodi, Carlo. *The Adventures of Pinocchio*. Originally published 1883. Available from Amazon.com.

Dumas, Alexandre, père. *The Count of Monte Cristo*. Originally published by Chapman and Hall, 1844. Available from Penguin Classics.

Dr. Seuss (Theodor Seuss Geisel). 1957. *How the Grinch Stole Christmas!* New York: Random House.

Lee, Harper. 1960. *To Kill a Mockingbird*. New York: J.B. Lippincott & Co.

Moffett, James and Betty Jane Wagner. 1976. *Student-Centered Language Arts and Reading, K-13: A Handbook for Teachers*. Boston, Mass.: Houghton Mifflin Company.

Ryan, Pam Munoz. 2002. *When Marian Sang*. New York: Scholastic Press.

Steig, William. 1985. *Abel's Island*. New York: Farrar, Straus & Giroux.

Steig, William. 1986. *Brave Irene*. New York: Farrar, Straus & Giroux.

Steig, William. 1986. *Caleb and Kate*. New York: Farrar, Straus & Giroux.

Steig, William. 1992. *Amos and Boris*. New York: Farrar, Straus & Giroux.

Stevenson, Robert Louis. 1883. *Treasure Island*. Scotland: Cassell & Company Ltd.

Unsworth, Len. 2006. *E-literature for Children: Enhancing Digital Literacy Learning*. New York: Routledge Education, Taylor & Francis Group.

RESOURCES

Websites (accessed April 9, 2009)

Art of William Steig: <http://www.thejewishmuseum.org/site/pages/content/exhibitions/special/steig/steig_onlinefeature.html>

Author, Walter Dean Myers: <http://www.walterdeanmyers.net/>

Author, Mem Fox: <http://www.memfox.net/welcome.html>

Author, Page McBrier: <http://www.pagemcbrier.com/picturebooks.html>

Heifer International: Ending Hunger, Caring for the Earth: <http://www.heifer.org/>

International Children's Digital Library: <http://en.childrenslibrary.org/>

Appendix
Teaching Tools

Teaching Tools

Getting to Know the Technology

Kristin Main

When I started teaching, I had access to a computer with slide presentation software, and eventually I gained access to an LCD projector. I have been slowly adding to my technology collection in terms of products—and vocabulary. Now there are several pieces of equipment and software that I consider staples for my own teaching.

Slide presentation software

Most of us are familiar with slide presentation software. One of the most familiar software applications is Microsoft Office PowerPoint. Basically, slide programs allow you to advance images. The software can also support various forms of information in a single slide: titles, text, images, graphics, charts, tables, sounds, and videos. The more advanced settings allow users to draw from ready-to-use slide templates, where information is plugged into pre-existing formats. Slides can be advanced using animation. This means you can select different effects as the slides play, including how the slides advance, how quickly they advance, and what sound effects will accompany the advance. Advancing slides can be automatic, set to a timer. Other features enable users to highlight text, add captions, even pre-record narration.

Scanner

A scanner optically scans an object and converts it into a digital file. The most common form of scanner is the desktop scanner, also referred to as a flatbed. There are hand-held models that are moved over top of the image, but the ease of use and portability of the desktops are proving to be the more popular choice.

Most scanners connect to the computer by a USB (universal serial bus) interface to save the image scanned. Scanners are generally operated in one of two manners (some scanners offer both) either through function buttons located on the scanner or a tool box that is displayed on your computer screen. Images may be saved as a single image or as a series of images. Most scanners actually scan into the TIFF format (tagged image file format) but allow you to save as a variety of other options such as JNG (JPEG network graphics) and PNG (portable network graphics). One of the most familiar formats is PDF (portable document format). The PDF format was created by Adobe as a means of viewing a fixed layout. Acrobat Reader, also created by Adobe, is needed to view PDF files. Scanners have become an affordable means of saving images.

Screen capture software

Screen capture software is just that—the ability to capture the image on the computer screen. Basically, this allows a picture to be taken of whatever is on the screen. Most software programs allow the user to select the capture method. The isolation of the object can be traced freehand; it can be selected by a predetermined shape placed over the areas of interest; it can be of the entire screen (also known as *wysiwyg—what you see is what you get—*and pronounced "wizzy wig") or of multiple selected areas of the screen; or videos and animations can be recorded.

Once the image is recorded it can be edited. This means the size, colour, and edge effects can be altered. Text can be added, objects inserted, or freehand drawings included. The software then allows for a variety of sharing options to save, print, or cut and paste the image into a new file or program. Many of the programs allow for the newly created image to be emailed or directly exported into the program of your choice.

The three most common ways to save the images are as JPEG, GIF, and PNG files. JPEG, standing for "joint photographic experts group," is a means of compressing photographic images. GIF, standing for "graphic interchange format," allows a user to take a larger amount of information from the image; however, images take up a lot of computer memory so a GIF image takes up a lot of space to include the information contained in all the colours of a picture. You will learn to make the trade-off between JPEG files, which use less memory, and GIF files, which give more detail. PNG, standing for "portable network graphics," is a method of mapping the information that creates an image. It is intended to be used in copying images rather than in producing professional quality photographs. It, like JPEG, is format free for use, while GIF is licensed. For basic usage, JPEG files will meet most of the basic needs.

When facing the many options in software programs, remember that "more expensive is not always best." Screen capture software programs are available for download at no charge other than the producer's request to tell your friends about the product. Be sure to note whether the software is offered with a lifetime licence, that is, a one-time fee, or whether you have to renew the licence so that the software will not expire—stop working—after a set period of time, usually 30 days or 1 year).

Some key features of interest are:
- screen capture options: select object, screen or multiple sections of the screen
- paint tools, edge effects, drawing tools, colour and size
- sharing methods that include save, print, cut and paste, and export
- no attached spyware (a program that collects data from the computer on which it is installed about such items as sites visited on the Internet and reports back to the company)
- no attached adware (advertisements included in the software or advertisements that the software downloads to the computer while it is running).

Digital camera

The cost of digital cameras has come down significantly over the past few years. The main features to look for as basic are
- an optical zoom x3—An optical zoom magnifies the area of focus with the lens, which produces a much sharper image than a digital zoom. The digital zoom enlarges the area of focus—like blowing up an image on the photocopier, which results in lower quality images.
- 2.5" LCD display screen—This size should allow most people to comfortably preview their images.
- 5 megapixels—A megapixels is the unit of measuring pixels, the smallest unit of the picture elements of an image.
- USB interface—This "universal serial bus" is the means by which peripherals, like a digital camera, are connected directly to the computer to use programs for viewing, editing, and printing the images captured.

Memory capacity is an important consideration when selecting a digital camera. Most digital cameras have 16 MB of internal memory. A digital photograph may contain between 150 KB to over 10 MB of memory, depending on its format, so 16 MB of internal memory will store between 2 and 15 photos. However, the internal memory shouldn't ultimately be a major consideration because you can purchase external memory, usually as a memory stick to insert into the camera. Again, the price for external memory is rapidly decreasing—for about the price for developing two rolls of film, you can buy 1 GB of memory, which would store approximately 650 pictures (depending on the memory needed for each picture). Digital photos can be downloaded to a computer or burned on to CDs or DVDs.

Many digital cameras also offer video recording, although videos use more memory. But you can set up the camera to take video just as you would shoot a picture—a very user-friendly way to capture sound and motion. A 10-second clip uses approximately 3 MB of memory. For longer videos or anything that needs a sharper production quality, a video camera is preferable.

MP3 Player

MP3 players are digital audio players (DAP), whose main functions are to play, store, and organize sound files. The full name is MPEG-layer 3, a file format allowing the user to compress digital audio data. Although the function of MP3 players is similar, the price range is very wide. The most notable brand name is Apple's iPod.

For classroom use, the following features are practical:
- USB interface—allows you to transfer files to and from a computer or other piece of technology.
- LCD screen—allows you to access menus, view titles of works, and control such features as volume and functions.
- Voice recorder—allows you to use an external microphone, which increases recording flexibility.
- 1 GB memory—As a refresher, there are 1000 kilobytes (KB) in a megabyte (MB) and 1000 megabytes in a gigabyte (GB). So 1 GB of memory can hold approximately 250 songs, each of which is about 4 minutes in length.

To determine how much memory you need, consider that a 2-minute song needs about 2 MB of memory, and a 10-minute voice recording also uses about 2 MB of memory. Through the USB interface, you can plug the MP3 player into your computer and manage its files; that is, you can transfer music files and audio recordings you make from your MP3 player to your computer and vice versa.

External speakers

Most recent computers have speakers, but for less than $15, you can invest in a pair of speakers that plug into the headphone jack of a computer. Look for speakers with volume control to take full advantage of sound effects, voice recordings, and music. However, less expensive speakers require their own power source, that is, an outlet to plug into. If you spend a few more dollars, you can invest in either battery-operated speakers and rechargeable batteries or speakers that draw power directly from your computer through the USB cable.

Teaching Tools

Using Microsoft Photo Story 3
Shirley Sinclair

Preparation

Prior to beginning, you will need to save images and sounds to a folder ready for use.

Images

You can use photographs from a digital camera, illustrations that you have scanned, or images saved from the Internet. Files that can be used include *.png, *.jpg, *.jpeg, *.tif, *.tiff, *.psd, *.eps, *.gif, *pcx, *.png, *.tga, *.bmp, *.dib, *.rle

To save an image from the Internet
1. Place your cursor on the image you would like to save and right click the mouse.
2. Select **Save Picture (image) As**.
3. Select the folder you would like to store your image in and click **Save**.

Sounds

Sounds may be found on the Internet, or you may like to save a copy of a song from CD onto your disk. (As a starting point, use <www.findsounds.com> or <http://www.freeplaymusic.com/index.php>.)

Files that can be imported into photo story are *.mpg, *.wav, and *.wma. Any other file types will need to be converted to one of the above.

To save a sound file from the Internet
1. Place your cursor on the sound file and right click the mouse.
2. Select **Save Target As**.
3. Select the folder you would like to store your sound file in and click **Save**.

Begin

1. Open Microsoft Photo Story 3 from the computer.
2. Select **Begin a new story**.
3. Select **Next**.

Importing Pictures

1. Click **Import Pictures**.

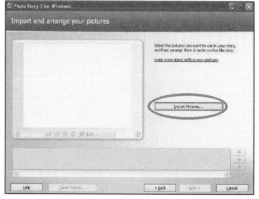

Locate the images

1. Navigate to the folder containing the images.
2. Select the images to use by holding Ctrl and click.
3. Click **OK**.

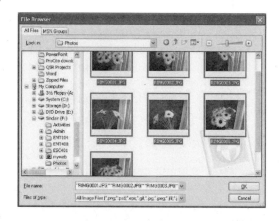

Arranging your pictures

The pictures selected are highlighted on the film strip.

They can now be edited and rearranged.

To **rearrange** or **delete** an image, click the image to be moved and use the arrow keys or the X to change the position. This can be done at any stage.

To **edit** click the edit button.

Editing your pictures

Rotate and Crop (tab) individual images
1. Tick the crop box.
2. Adjust the frame by dragging the handles.
3. Click **Next** if completed editing.
4. To continue editing, click the tab for **Auto Fix** or **Add Effect**.

Auto Fix tab
Select the areas to adjust (note that it has selected the cropped picture).

Add Effect tab
Choose the effect you want to apply from the choice of effects.

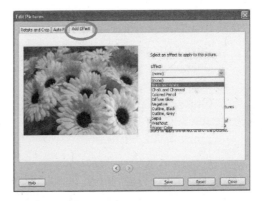

Choose whether to apply the effect to all pictures or to this picture only.

Save

Click **Save** to return to the storyboard or click one of the arrows to select another picture to edit.

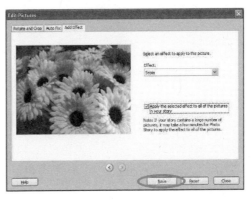

When you have finished editing all pictures click **Next**.

Adding text to pictures

You may wish to add names, dates, titles, quotes, etc.
1. Select the picture to which you want to add text.
2. The effect can also be adjusted at this stage.
3. Type your text into the textbox.

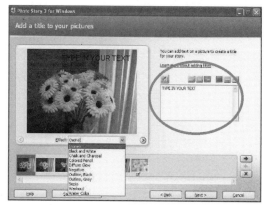

1. Select the font and characteristics by clicking the **A** button.
2. Adjust the position and spacing by clicking the appropriate button.

3. Continue adding text to individual pictures by selecting them on the filmstrip. Once you have completed adding text to all your pictures, select **Next**.

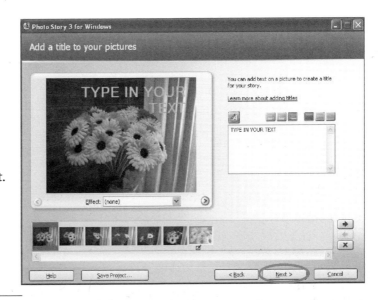

Customizing a Motion Path

This step allows you to pan in and out of your pictures. Select how and where you would like the panning to occur.

1. Select **Customize Motion**.

2. From the **Motion and Duration** tab, tick **Specify start and end position of motion** (or you can leave it set automatically).
3. Two copies of your picture are presented. The first one is titled **Start position** and the second identical image **End position**: Both images have a box that can be repositioned by dragging the resize handles. If you want your picture to show the full view and then zoom in to a specific spot, you leave the **Start Position** image as is and adjust the size and position of the box on the second image to suit. Alternatively, you may like to start in close-up and pan out. Once you have made your choice, select **Save**.
4. Use the arrow button to move on and adjust your next image. Once you have adjusted the panning properties for all images select the **Transition** tab.

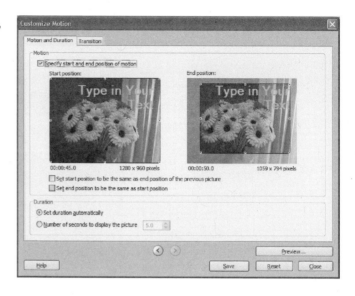

The Transition menu allows you to select an effect that will be played as your images move from one picture to the next.

1. Make your selection and click **Save**.
2. Once you are happy with the transition effects you have selected for your presentation, click **Close**.

Note: To remove the black screen from the start of the Photo Story, remove the tick from **Start current picture using a transition**.

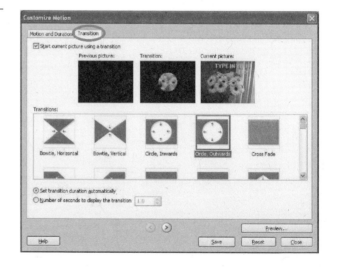

Recording Narration

Before recording your narration, ensure that your microphone is plugged in, switched on, and configured. To help with your narration, you may like to type your text into the prompt box. This allows you to read from the screen while recording.

1. Click the red record button and begin speaking.
2. Once you have recorded the information for the first picture, it is a good idea to hit the stop button, select Preview and listen to your recording.
3. Continue recording the narration to accompany each picture. Remember to speak clearly and slowly.

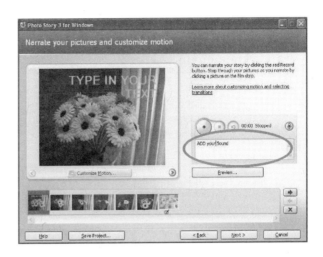

Adding Sound and Music Files

1. Highlight the picture where you would like the music to begin playing.
2. Click **Select Music** and locate your saved music or sound file from your folder.
3. Click **Create Music** to use music from the program.
4. Click **Delete Music** to remove music.

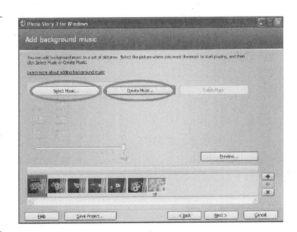

Create Music

1. Choose music to suit your presentation from the properties of genre, style, and bands.
2. Adjust Tempo and Intensity (if applicable).
3. Click **Play** arrow to hear the sound.
4. Note that file size may be increased if you use Create Music.
5. Select **Silence** to create a pause in the music, particularly if narration is used on a picture.

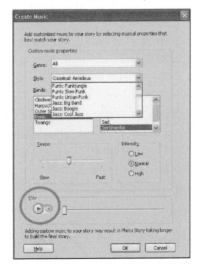

Preview

1. Adjust the volume to ensure that the music is complementary without drowning out the narration.
2. Select **Preview** to ensure that everything is exactly how you want it.

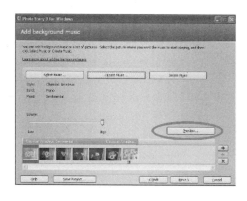

Moving Back and Forwards

- At any stage, by clicking the **Back** button, you can return to the beginning screen of **Import and arrange your pictures**.
- At any stage, by clicking the **Next** button, you can move forward.

Save your project

1. Select **Save Project**.
2. Select a folder on your drive.
3. Saving your work as a project allows you to reopen this file to make further adjustments to your presentation.
4. It is saved as a *.wp3 file.
5. Click **Next**.

Save your story

This saves the Photo Story as a *.wmv file to be played through Windows Media Player.

1. Select what you want to do with your story from the list of options.
2. Choose a location on your drive to save your story by clicking **Browse**.
3. Click **Settings**.

Choose the most appropriate size. The default is **Profile for Computers 2**, but **Profile for Computers 1** may be more appropriate as it is a smaller file.

Click **OK**.

Click **Next**.

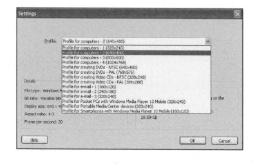

Your story will be saved to your folder as a *.wmv file.

At the completion of the save process, you will be asked if you would like to view your story or begin a new story.

Or you can Exit the program.

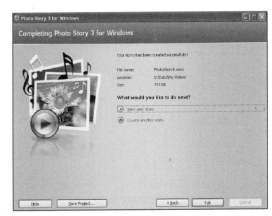

REFERENCES

Microsoft Site

<http://www.microsoft.com/windowsxp/using/digitalphotography/photostory/tips/firststory.mspx>

<http://www.microsoft.com/windowsxp/using/digitalphotography/photostory/tips/create.mspx>

Contributors

DEIRDRE BAKER has taught children's literature at various universities in Canada and the USA and is currently an Assistant Professor in the Department of English at the University of Toronto. She is co-author with Ken Setterington of *A Guide to Canadian Children's Books* (McClelland & Stewart 2003) and author of the children's novel *Becca at Sea* (Groundwood Books 2007), which was a Horn Book Fanfare selection for 2007 and named among the top ten children's books of the year. Deirdre Baker has been the children's book reviewer for the *Toronto Star* since 1998, and she writes and reviews regularly for *Quill & Quire* and *The Horn Book Journal*.

When **JANE BASKWILL** was a child, her parents allowed her to write on one wall of her bedroom. It was in this space that she published, in words and pictures, her first stories and launched her writing self. Now, as a teacher educator at Mount Saint Vincent University, she brings the arts, children's literature, and her interest in new media and new literacies to her work with teachers and administrators. She is intrigued and excited by the possibilities that the merger of old and new technologies affords our teaching and learning.

KIMBERLY BEZAIRE is an Early Childhood Education specialist and doctoral candidate at the Ontario Institute for Studies in Education, University of Toronto. Her research and writing interests include children's classroom play, multiliteracies, and the children's toy market. Having taught in early years settings, as a teacher educator, she consults on projects relating to kindergarten and the arts in early childhood. Kimberly enjoys bike riding, playing and googling on the computer with her eight-year-old son.

From his beginnings as a reader at the public library in Sarnia, **David Booth** has spent his life among books for children and young adults—as a teacher reading them aloud, as a consultant bringing them to schools, as a professor talking about their strengths and possibilities, as a parent sharing them with his son, and as a writer telling stories and finding poems that kids will enjoy. He continues his passion for children's literature by writing about texts in all their forms, and by buying books to read to his granddaughter.

Oh, the stories that **Linda Cameron** composed as a child when romping through the forest, daydreaming by a brook, or teaching all the naughty scholars in her pretend classroom! Toys were texts full of meaning and potential. Now, media expand the possibilities by opening up new worlds and inquiries, answering many questions but inviting more, and connecting us. Wow! As a teacher of every age, a parent of three, a teacher educator, and a researcher, Linda is thankful that she has been able to play with the many kinds of text and with play partners, here and around the world, who have helped develop her stories and ideas.

Elana Shapiro Davidson, who completed her MED at OISE, University of Toronto, has taught for ten years in primary classrooms. She enjoys watching her students experience stories on paper as well as interacting with text on screen. Elana secretly dreams of one day having a SMART Board mounted on her kitchen wall, and her greatest joy is telling her two children "Lights out" but allowing them to stay up just five more minutes because they are curled up in bed reading books in print and onscreen!

Miriam Davidson is Assistant Professor and Coordinator of Integrated Arts at Trent University in Ontario. Her research focuses on the role of the arts in enhancing student engagement in learning, the connection between the production of visual imagery (photography in particular) and student literacy, and the artistic practices and traditions in non-formal, community-based settings. Her qualitative studies bring underserved communities of learners together with pre-service teachers and artists through arts enrichment outreach and service learning projects.

Brenda Stein Dzaldov is in the third year of a PHD program at OISE/UT. She is a teacher and literacy consultant, specializing in the areas of Reading Recovery™, ESL, and Special Education. Brenda has written levelled children's literature for classroom reading instruction and published professional articles, both locally and internationally, with a specific focus on text and new literacies. She is the mother of three children—Jenny, Mitchell, and Benji—with whom she has experienced and loved a wide range of children's literature over the past 14 years.

Naomi Hamer is a PhD candidate at the Centre for Children, Youth and Media at the Institute of Education, University of London, UK. She has an MA in Children's Literature from the University of British Columbia, and has worked extensively as a drama and creative arts instructor in schools, libraries, and recreational centres. Her recent focus is on the development of programs for young people that use digital technologies to engage with children's literature.

Carol Jupiter is a classroom teacher in Toronto, Ontario. Her love of books, words, and writing began when her mother took Carol on weekly ventures to a tiny library a long time ago. Today she shares this love with her family, friends, and students. In this realm she has the time and opportunity to delve into text and the magic of reading.

Mary Ladky currently teaches at Trent University's School of Education and Professional Learning. Her teaching and research areas include secondary English studies, sociocultural perspectives on the teaching of English, and supporting special-needs learners. Before obtaining her doctorate, Dr. Ladky taught English and literature studies in Beijing, Hong Kong, Montreal, and New York. She is married to the Canadian author, Charles Foran, and they live with their two daughters—and a proliferating collection of books for young and old—in Peterborough, Ontario.

Heather Lotherington teaches in Education and Linguistics at York University in Toronto. She has been involved in researching multiliteracies at Joyce Public School in northwest Toronto since 2003, when she spent a sabbatical year at Joyce observing classes, volunteering as an ESL assistant, and reading stories to kindergarten children. Since then, she has worked actively and continuously both with the teachers to design multiliteracy pedagogies that include digital media, contemporary genres, and community languages in emergent literacy education for urban, multicultural children, and with the principal to create a learning community that facilitates research-based professional development.

Margaret Mackey is a professor in the School of Library and Information Studies at the University of Alberta. She teaches and researches in the area of multimodal and print literacies, and also teaches young adult literature. Her most recent book is *Mapping Recreational Literacies: Contemporary Adults at Play* (Lang 2007), and she has published numerous articles on the breathtaking changes in the literate behaviours and tastes of contemporary young people.

Leslie McGrath studied at the University of Toronto, completing an MLS degree in 1984 and, in 2005, a PhD in Information Studies, a collaborative program in book history and print culture. She has been with the Toronto Public Library as head of the Osborne Collection of Early Children's Books since 1995.

Kristin Main, a former secondary school English teacher with Lakehead District School Board in Northwestern Ontario, was amazed by the technological abilities of students. She was even more amazed by their abilities to adapt to and develop with the ever-changing face of the digital world. It was because of them that she returned to her own studies, enrolling as a doctoral candidate at OISE, University of Toronto, where she is currently investigating ways to learn from the students' experiences and connect them with the realities of being socially aware consumers and producers of varied texts.

Jamie Campbell Naidoo is an Endowed Assistant Professor at the University of Alabama's School of Library and Information Studies. He has served on numerous national (American) and international book awards committees, including the Caldecott. When he is not teaching and researching in the areas of diversity in libraries and children's literature, Jamie spends his time restoring his 1940s bungalow and enjoying a good cup of coffee with his fearless Siamese, Kiki.

Shelley Stagg Peterson is an associate professor at OISE, University of Toronto. Her research and teaching in writing, writing assessment, and children's literature are grounded in eight years of teaching in elementary schools in rural Alberta. In 2001, she founded the Toronto Reading Council, which sponsored the "Place for Children's Literature in New Literacies Classrooms" conference. She is returning to her rural roots in her research, asking questions about teaching literacy in isolated rural communities, and enjoying country life in eastern Ontario with her husband and cat every weekend, come rain, snow, or sunshine.

Ken Setterington is a librarian, storyteller, author, and reviewer. He is the Children and Youth Advocate for Library Services at the Toronto Public Library. In 2000, he was named the Librarian of the Year by the Ontario Library Association. He co-wrote *A Guide to Canadian Children's Books in English* (McClelland & Stewart 2003) with Deirdre Baker. Ken is an acknowledged expert on children's and teen literature and has served on award committees for the TD Canadian Children's Literature Award, the Newbery Medal, and the Caldecott Medal. He can be heard on CBC Radio discussing the best new books for children as a member of the Children's Book Panel.

Shirley Sinclair has lectured in Information and Communication Technologies for seven years in the School of Education at Charles Sturt University in Wagga Wagga, New South Wales, Australia. Prior to this appointment she was a teacher-librarian and computer coordinator at a primary school in Wagga Wagga.

JEANETTE THOMPSON once made Polkaroo fly over the CN Tower on Imagination Day. She also wrote scripts for Polka Dot Shorts, Mr. Dressup, and Playschool before returning to Australia to teach as a Reading Recovery™ specialist. Currently, she lectures in multiliteracies and children's literature in the School of Education, Charles Sturt University. She hopes to encourage her pre-service teachers, and their students, to fly with digital texts. Cyberwriters are the authors of the future.

Notes

Notes